Professionalism and Sustainability in the Professional Associations Sector:
UK and Ireland

Andrew Friedman
with
Nataliya Afitska

ISBN: 978-0-9545487-6-6

Contents

Chapter 4 - Employment, management and operations   **57**

Chapter 5 - Income and diversification of income   **91**

Chapter 6 - Membership issues   **109**

Chapter 7 - Member relations   **129**

List of figures and tables

Figures

Tables

List of case studies

Acknowledgements

As with all major PARN research projects, many contribute.

We would like to thank all the professional bodies in the UK and Ireland who took the time to answer what was a very long and detailed questionnaire. We would especially like to thank those that agreed to be interviewed for case studies.

This book also draws information from contributions to the PARN Members Enquiry system. We would like to thank all who answered enquiries, and particularly those that regularly answer these enquiries. You provide much of the illumination that is essential for the professional associations 'sector' collectively to reflect on its practice.

There are many staff at PARN who have contributed to this book. We would like to thank Susannah Woodhead and Emily Pickering for carrying out and preparing case studies for this book. We would also like to thank Christina Williams and Jane Mason for their work on the design of the questionnaire and for support with editing this book, Xiaojie (Lin) Kirby for her work on the cover design, Brett Lambe for proof reading, and Elizabeth Sheeran for work on foundation documents of professional associations. Finally we would like to thank Julia Denman for general support for the book and particularly for organising and carrying out the final proof reading and style checking.

Andy Friedman & Nataliya Afitska
March 2007

Preface

This book builds on work carried out since PARN was founded in 1998. The ideas explored here are broad and fundamental to the future for the professions: progress on the professionalisation of professional associations, linking this to the concept of their sustainability and discerning strategies to support their sustainable development, and viewing professional associations as a sector, with its implications for awareness of what is common in their aims, their situation, their activities, and particularly what they can learn from each other in fulfilling their role and sustaining their accomplishments.

At the heart of this book is information gathered through new comprehensive surveys of professional associations carried out in 2006 in the UK and Ireland. These surveys are closely matched to comprehensive surveys carried out by PARN in 2003, providing a unique opportunity to monitor the progress of many associations who responded to both surveys. In addition the book is supported by case studies and small-scale surveys and enquiries carried out by PARN in the past few years.

PARN is a 'research-enriched network' providing thought and knowledge leadership for professional associations. It is also a membership organisation with over 140 professional associations belonging to PARN in the UK, Ireland, Canada and Australia. PARN carries out and publishes research, holds networking events, and provides advice to its members on subjects of concern to professionals and particularly to professional associations. The subjects we deal with include: governance and management of professional associations, membership, member relations and member services, continuing professional development, ethical codes, complaints and disciplinary procedures, and educational supports for the ethical competence of professionals.

The PARN website (http://www.parn.org.uk) provides information about our work and our publications.

- Chapter 1 -
Background, themes and empirical base

1.1   Background

This book builds on work carried out over the past 9 years at PARN. It particularly builds on comprehensive surveys of professional associations[1] in the UK and Ireland undertaken in 2003 and reported in two previous PARN publications (Friedman and Mason, 2004a; Friedman and Mason, 2004b). At the heart of this book is information gathered through new comprehensive surveys of professional associations carried out in 2006. A majority of questions in the 2006 surveys are identical with those of the 2003 surveys. This provides a unique opportunity to examine changes over the past three years in a substantial number of professional associations that responded to both surveys.

Professional associations have developed over the past three years. Pressures on them have continued unabated, stimulated particularly by the spread of Internet usage and by continuing fallout from high profile scandals such as ENRON/Arthur Andersen, Parmalat, Shipman and various financial services transgressions. The media is now much more sensitive to disciplinary cases, particularly in the health and financial services sectors. In addition there are continuing government initiatives, both from the UK, Ireland and the EU to 'marketise' services and services labour markets. Professional associations are being pressed to react to these pressures. In this book we present evidence for how professional associations are changing, as well as providing some overarching concepts or themes which we believe will help professional

---

[1] A note on terminology: We generally use the term 'professional associations' to refer to a wide range of professional bodies that include both pure professional associations (representing and supporting individuals in their capacity as professionals), plus organisations that combine the function of professional associations with other functions concerned with professionals and the professions; such as, learned societies, regulatory bodies, awarding bodies, trade unions and trade associations. See Chapter 2 for further elaboration of this distinction.

associations to react positively to these pressures, both individually and collectively.

Three particular themes dominate this book:

- The professionalisation of professional associations. This builds directly on the main theme of the publications of 2004.

- Sustainability of professional associations. This has been dealt with in passing in previous publications and, in particular, diversification of income streams was dealt with briefly in the two publications of 2004. Here this issue is explored explicitly and more consistently in relation to a wider set of practices.

- Viewing of professional associations (in addition to other professional bodies such as regulatory bodies and learned societies) as a sector in its own right. This theme has been mentioned in a number of previous PARN publications, but explored more explicitly here. To consider professional associations as representing a sector, to develop propositions about that sector as a whole and to make recommendations for improving the practice of all organisations in that sector may be regarded as the underlying basis for PARN research. PARN is dedicated to the idea that professional associations can all learn from each other and that serial benchmarking across the professions can be valuable to all parts of the sector. Professional associations are complex organisations. Even if some associations are 'ahead' of the majority for certain practices, they are likely to benefit from exposure to 'interesting' practice and 'good' practice elsewhere in the sector, in relation to other issues.

1.2 Professionalisation of professional associations

The primary theme of the previous PARN publications was to evaluate the proposition that professional associations in the UK and Ireland were becoming 'more strategic, more flexible, more reflective, in short, more professional.' (Friedman and Mason, 2004a: 140). This is a way of viewing the reaction of professional associations to the well-known pressures on them. Professionalisation of professional associations as a proposition was primarily investigated in the UK at that time.[2] It was found that there was movement in this direction on many fronts, but that it was 'patchy' with a minority making substantial changes to their practice in any one aspect of their practice, and that the numbers making changes were different for different broad categories of their practice. Associations were changing at different 'speeds' in relation to different broad categories of their own practice. Overall we found more evidence for professionalisation in relation to member relations, income diversification and a more strategic approach to management and employment, but less in streamlining and focusing governance structures to deliver more strategic guidance to associations. We found use of more formal reflective methods was associated with the size of associations.

In comparison with the UK, Irish associations were found to be more traditional in their governance, also there seemed to be less of a labour market in Ireland for jobs in professional associations. Associations were more likely to be run by someone with a professional qualification from the association, rather than management qualifications or experience of managing other professional associations. (Friedman and Mason, 2004b, 56-57). However there were a number of areas where Irish professional associations were further 'advanced' in professionalisation, particularly when size of association is taken into account. For example Irish associations were less reliant on member subscriptions than those in the UK (Friedman and Mason, 2004b: 52). This may be due to Irish associations being more influenced by the practices of larger associations elsewhere (possibly in the UK, but also from the USA). This is a proposition that needs further investigation.

---

[2] PARN began in the UK in 1998 and had access to materials concerning the organisation of professional bodies in the UK from 1990 onwards. PARN only established a significant presence in Ireland in May 2002 with its first event there and PARN research in Ireland only really began with the 2003 survey. In that survey Irish professional bodies were compared with those in the UK, rather than comparing the current position in Ireland with past situations.

1.3 Sustainability and professional associations

Sustainability is a concept that can be used to examine how professional associations are developing from a new perspective. On one hand, it suggests that economic stability needs to be tempered with social stability and that the environment of associations, not only their connection to the natural environment, but also their influence on the economy, society and the environment as a sector in an ecological context, needs to be considered. On the other hand, it also suggests that the complexity of professional associations themselves, in terms of associations having multiple objectives, and therefore multiple 'bottom lines', needs to be taken into account when considering how associations should be organised. Especially when considering how management and operational techniques that are designed for private sector organisations, may need to be altered in order to make them appropriate for professional associations.

These issues are important when professional associations consider risk assessment and risk management. In the context of risk as well as long term strategy, the way associations approach the membership and member relations is particularly important. However in Chapter 2 we also consider some strategies that are based on more positive and proactive aspects of the concept of sustainability.

1.4 Professional associations as a sector

Pressures on professionals from more demanding and less trusting clients, pressures from employers who are increasingly inclined to take a more aggressive managerial approach to the professionals in their employ, pressures on professionals from increasing likelihood of being taken to court for malpractice, pressures from tighter government regulation and the overall pressure of a change in public attitude towards professionals stimulated by media interest in instances of malpractice; all lead professionals to expect more from their professional associations. Also, the general change in attitude of consumers towards companies selling all sorts of goods and services, stimulated by the rise of consumerism in the 1970s and 1980s, and by the response of companies to this and to the challenge of rising international competition, particularly from Japan which is symbolised by the quality movement of the 1980s and 1990s, may be said to have changed attitudes towards any organisation providing goods or services. The expectation of receiving value for money for any market transaction for goods or services, spills over to members expecting value for money in some sense for their subscription fees, as well as for any goods or services that professional associations expect their members to pay for separately.

In addition, the present government's active and interventionist approach to regulation has led to challenges to the traditional role of self-regulation. Even where a strong organisational separation has been made between professional associations as representatives of their members and regulatory bodies, the line between these functions can waver depending on government policy and policy decisions by the respective organisations.

These problems are felt to varying degrees across traditionally defined sectors that would normally divide professional associations. However, we are finding that professional associations are more open to benchmarking themselves across those traditionally defined sectors. Attendance at PARN events and membership of PARN crosses all these traditional sectors. We detect an increasing acceptance among professional associations that they are in a common situation and one that is distinguishable from others. In effect, professional associations are coming to see themselves as belonging to an identifiable sector of the economy and society.

Viewing professional associations as a sector primarily encourages an interest among organisations within the sector to discover how others are dealing with the pressures noted above. PARN regularly presents cases of interesting practice in its publications and several such cases are presented in this book. In other PARN publications we have emphasised particular aspects of the practice of professional associations, particularly in the UK, that encourage them to see themselves as being in the same sector. In particular we have produced books that associations in terms of their development of CPD policies and programmes over the past 20 years (Friedman et al, 2000; Friedman 2005), changes in routes to membership (Friedman, Phillips and Cruickshank, 2002), governance structures and processes (Friedman Phillips and Chan, 2002; Friedman and Phillips, 2003; Friedman and Mason, 2006), and changes in strategic member relations (Friedman and Williams, 2006). This book concentrates on a wide range of practices of professional associations - employment, management, operations, income, membership and member relations –

in order to provide a more comprehensive picture of professional associations as a sector.

1.5 Empirical base: surveys

1.5.1 Introduction

We consider the survey results reported in this book to indicate the situation of the whole sector of professional associations. However the two sets of surveys carried out in 2003 and 2006, like almost all surveys, contain information directly about only those professional associations in the two countries that responded to the questionnaires. We report the results of these surveys as indicating the situation of the whole sector. The quality of our generalisations to create statements describing the professional associations sector depends on several factors:

- How comprehensive is the database information on the population of professional associations at PARN?

- How representative of the population of associations is the sample of those that responded to the survey?

- How clear were the questions asked? How well understood were they?

- How well do the responses given to the questions reflect the reality at each of the respondent professional associations? How well do respondents understand their association?

All of these factors are issues common to the validity claims for the results of any survey. We do not claim that the information in this book provides a perfect view of the state of professional associations in the UK and Ireland in 2006, and we know it can be improved. However, we do claim that this is the most comprehensive view of this sector ever produced in the UK or Ireland.

1.5.2 Responses

Between April and July 2006 110 useable responses were received to the 334 questionnaires sent out as part of the 2006 PARN survey into the Professionalisation of Professional Associations in the UK. A similar survey was sent to 114 professional associations in Ireland in June and by December 2006, 21 useable responses had been received. These surveys are being replicated in Canada and Australia and responses to these surveys will be compared with material published here in publications that will appear later in 2007.

The 2006 survey builds upon a comparable survey carried out in 2003 in the UK and Ireland.[3] Several questions have been altered, some questions have been added and some dropped, reflecting the development of our knowledge of the sector at PARN and reactions to the answers given in 2003. In most of the sections of this book, where the questions have been the same in both surveys, reference will be made to how the answers to questions in the two surveys compare for the group of associations that responded to those questions in both surveys. This allows us to address the issue of changes in the overall process of professionalisation of professional associations over time more confidently than we could address them in the analysis of the 2003 survey.

The 2003 UK survey was sent to 299 professional associations and 129 useable responses were received while the 2003 Irish survey was sent to 114 professional associations and 25 useable responses were received. There were 61 professional associations that responded to both the 2003 and the 2006 surveys in the UK and 15 responded to both in Ireland.

1.5.3   PARN database

PARN regularly attempts to 'prove' its database, telephoning to ensure that email addresses and names of associations are correct and keeping track of changes in the sector due to mergers. It is more difficult to keep track of new associations and break-away organisations, which are continually arising. We therefore would caution the reader that the estimation of the population of associations from our database will less comprehensively represent the actual population for the smallest of professional associations (those with under 1000 members).

---

[3] The Irish survey was open for respondents between September and December 2003; the UK survey between June 2003 and February 2004.

7

1.5.4   Representivity

The population of associations sent the questionnaire was higher in 2006 than in 2003 in the UK (334 as opposed to 299) reflecting efforts by PARN to identify all organisations in the sector. However this is less than the 400+ estimate we used for the population in the past before we undertook a comprehensive survey. The lowering of our estimate of the population is due to finding that many associations that we had considered to be professional associations were in fact purely trade associations. The Irish survey was sent to the same number of associations in 2006 compared with 2003 (114).

We received 112 responses to the UK survey representing a 33% response rate. We rejected two of the responses based on them being purely trade associations. The 21 responses to the Irish survey, all of which were accepted as professional associations, represents a 18% response rate. The differential response rate reflects the fact that PARN is clearly less well, and more recently, established in Ireland. This, and the relatively low absolute number of Irish responses leads us to have less confidence in providing results for Ireland. However, from the analysis presented in Friedman and Mason, 2004b, we are aware of systematic differences in responses to the questionnaire according to size of association. We therefore present some, but more limited information on these features of the survey for Ireland compared with the UK. Tables 1:1 and 1:2 provide some information on the difference in size and sector between samples and population for the UK and Irish surveys.

1.5.5 Size of respondents compared with size of associations in the population

Table 1:1 Size of professional associations: UK vs. Ireland

	Number of individual members					
	1-500	501-1500	1501-5000	5001-20000	>20000	Total
UK sample	8%	14%	28%	27%	23%	102[1]
UK population	7%	11%	32%	32%	19%	255[2]
Irish sample	16%	37%	37%	11%	0%	19[3]
Irish population	23%	32%	29%	14%	3%	66[4]

[1] Difference from 110 due to non response to the question about number of individual members.
[2] Difference from 334 due to lack of information about number of individual members.
[3] Difference from 21 due to non response to the question about number of individual members.
[4] Difference from 114 due to lack of information about number of individual members.

1.5.6 (Sub)Sector of respondents compared with population (sub)sectors

Sector distribution for respondents

Eighteen sectors were specified and respondents were asked to tick the one which best described the field of expertise that their association represents. The sectors were offered in alphabetical order. These are displayed in Table 1:2 in grouped order. The second column, 'Detailed sector', shows the set of 17 possible 'sectors' offered in the questionnaire. The final sector offered was 'other'. The allocation of respondents to these sectors indicated by the respondents themselves was used, unless they chose 'other'. The three associations that chose 'other' were allocated to specified sectors by PARN. The 'Group sector' column was assembled based on our understanding of how associations would group themselves.

Table 1:2   Sector distribution of the sample: UK and Ireland

Group sector	Detailed sector	% Detailed UK	% Group UK	% Group Ireland
	Medical/health	21%		
	Public services	5%		
	Welfare/social	2%		
Health & social			**28%**	**23%**
	Accountancy	7%		
	Business/management	11%		
	Finance	6%		
	Law	1%		
	Marketing/PR	3%		
Finance, law business & management			**29%**	**31%**
	Agriculture/environment	7%		
	Engineering	11%		
	Science	6%		
	Surveying/construction	5%		
	IT/communications	2%		
Engineering, science, environment & construction			**31%**	**31%**
	Media/publishing	2%		
	Arts/creative	2%		
	Culture/leisure	3%		
	Teaching/academia	6%		
Education, media & culture			**12%**	**15%**

The three main sectors for the professions have been grouped and represent fairly equal proportions of the sample, that is, 'health and social'; 'finance, law, business & management'; 'engineering, science, environment and construction'. The fourth group is more diverse, covering 'education, media & culture'. The UK and Irish samples are remarkably similar in the distribution across the four group sectors. Therefore differences in average responses between the two country samples are not likely to reflect sectoral differences among respondents.

Table 1:3 Broad (sub)sector distribution of respondents compared with the population: UK vs. Ireland

	Health & social	Finance, law, business, management	Engineering, science, environment, construction	Education, media, communi-cations, arts	Total
UK sample	27%	29%	30%	14%	110
UK population	28%	28%	28%	16%	334
Irish sample	24%	29%	33%	14%	21
Irish population	27%	27%	33%	12%	114

1.5.7   Clarity of survey questions

PARN has invested a lot of effort into the questions in the surveys. All questions from the 2003 survey were reviewed in the light of how well they were answered. Minor adjustments were made to some questions, some were dropped and new ones added. In addition the questionnaire was reviewed by a small number of PARN members. This has been repeated as the survey has gone into different national versions during 2006 (and early 2007 for the anticipated Australian version of the questionnaire). The questionnaire is still not 'perfect' in that some questions have been answered inconsistently by some respondents and some have been misinterpreted by some respondents. Generally, when this has occurred these answers have been re-coded as non-responses.

1.5.8   Quality of responses

The surveys that were returned were of reasonably high quality, given that the questionnaire was long and that questions were wide ranging. One consequence of this is that it would have been difficult for a single person to answer all questions accurately (for large associations) unless they consulted colleagues or unless several individuals from respondent associations filled out sections of the survey that called upon their specialist knowledge of how the association operates. This requires considerable good will and effort from the person to whom the survey was sent in the first instance.

PARN identifies a primary contact at all of its members and attempts to identify a potential primary contact at non-members on the database. In many instances the primary contact at a non-member association will be familiar with PARN through attending PARN conferences and workshops and/or through purchasing PARN books. The questionnaire was sent directly to these people, rather than to the associations without a named contact.

The level of non-responses was fairly low for such a complex and long questionnaire, on average there were 8.5 or 6% of non-responses over the 148 questions in the questionnaire.

1.6   Empirical base: other sources

Information about the professional associations from the surveys described above has been supplemented with information about the practice of professional associations in the UK and Ireland based on the PARN Member Enquiry system (see http://www.parn.org.uk) and from follow up telephone calls to explore interesting practice identified by qualitative answers to the questionnaire.

1.7   Outline structure of this book

In the next two chapters we examine two of the three broad themes introduced in Section 1.1 above, applying the concept of sustainability to professional associations and viewing the whole set of professional associations as a sector. In Chapter 4 we deal with topics covered in the survey in the area of management, employment and operations. Chapter 5 concerns income and particularly the diversification of income streams. Chapters 6 and 7 deal with membership and member relations respectively. In Chapter 8 we examine how the results of the surveys are affected by size, sector and growth. We end in Chapter 9 with conclusions based on a consideration of the primary themes raised in Section 1.2 above and provide some recommendations based on this research.

- Chapter 2 -
The sustainability and development of professional associations

2.1 Introduction

In the first half of this chapter we introduce the concept of sustainable development and derive some principles that can be applied to professional associations. We begin at the most general level with the sustainable development of the planet, with the underlying meaning of the concept of sustainable development and discern general principles for achieving sustainability from the underlying concept. We then examine the application of sustainability to specific organisations and then to individual professional associations. We argue that principles for sustainability can best be applied to complex entities and that professional associations are suitable cases for the application of these principles because they are complex entities in themselves. The nature of this complexity is then examined. It is due both to the different aims of professional associations, what may be labelled their multiple bottom lines, and also to the lack of centralised control over their own processes. The latter arises because of both their commitment to democratic representation of their members and their reliance on voluntary effort, particularly in governance, but also at many, for management control and operational functions. These features are not regarded as dysfunctional, rather they are complicating factors, which make the issue of sustainability relevant to professional associations even though the concept was designed to provide a useful perspective on much larger entities, such as societies or the whole planet.

In the second half of the chapter we deal with three broad strategies and processes for achieving sustainable development of professional associations. One of these broad strategies is well known: risk assessment and risk management. The other two strategies are new, or at least newly formulated in terms of broad strategies. They relate first, to the multiple bottom lines of professional associations, and second, to the environment or ecology of professional associations, which are implied by the multiple bottom lines. The latter we label as a strategy based on 'time-dependent ecological effects'. All the strategies are explained and justified. Examples of policies and actions that professional associations can pursue, which can be regarded as following these strategies, are provided.

2.2.   The concept of sustainable development

The concept of sustainable development may be used to analyse the situation of professional associations and to develop action recommendations for them. Sustainable development has become one of the most popular buzzwords of the past 20 years. As is the way with buzzwords, they come to mean different things to different people. A generally accepted definition is the original one offered by the World Commission on Environment and Development in 1987: *"Development that meets the needs of the present without compromising the ability of future generations to meet their own needs."* (PP4SD, 2001: 28). Sustainability is the goal of sustainable development. Sustainable development is often associated more specifically with what is often called triple bottom line goals; environmental, economic and social goals. Environmental goals concern the position of human life within its natural environment, how it draws on and shapes its surroundings, living and non-living, and particularly its use of natural resources. Economic goals concern the material well-being of the population, usually thought of in terms of economic growth and levels of employment. Social goals concern the ways people relate to each other, that there is development towards sustainable social relations thought of in terms of community relations in civil society and levels of conflict, with implications for the distribution of economic resources. The principles that have informed and are supported by this way of thinking may be thought of as involving three key principles:

- A *multiple perspective* on the impact of one's actions, in particular on more than just economic or social or environmental factors, but rather on them all and at the same time.

- A systems[4] or systematic or ecological[5] view of one's position and of the consequences of one's actions. Not only can actions affect the economic, social and environmental context of those taking actions, but also these *effects are interlinked and may take time to manifest themselves*. Influences on the economy, society and the environment can have secondary effects, thereby amplifying the consequences of actions on those taking actions (in most cases the human race is the class of agents of concern). Furthermore, these effects have further tertiary effects and so on, on both the surroundings and those taking actions. That is, the long term effects can be systematically different from short term effects. It is only by looking at all the elements and particularly how those elements inter-relate as a 'system' that these long term consequences of actions can be appreciated.

- Sustainable development is an *underspecified concept*, requiring further examination and reflection. While on the one hand it is recognised that one must take a systematic approach, on the other hand, there is not enough of an understanding of how the various elements and sub-systems connect with each other as part of the overall situation. The system depends on human actions as well as non-human factors and while there may be regularities in how people interact with each other and with their non-human environment, people have memories and their interactions develop in ways which means that however regular a pattern appears to occur, there will always be new emerging elements to the situation, if only because the experience of the past must always plough a unique furrow, even if there are familiar elements to it. This means that one cannot specify the system in all its detail; there will always be new elements and new patterns of interaction to it. Until this situation changes, (if indeed it could ever change) complacency is dangerous. Further reflection on what precisely sustainable development is will be necessary for the foreseeable future.

---

[4] A system is an organised or connected group of objects so as to form a complex unity (*Oxford English Dictionary*). A systems approach is intended to enable complex and dynamic situations to be broadly understood (*Oxford English Dictionary*).
[5] Ecology is the term originally used (from the late 19th century) as a branch of biology concerned with the relations of living organisms with their surroundings. It is derived from the Greek term *oikos* meaning household or living place (*Oxford English Dictionary*). Since the 1920s human ecology has developed in the social sciences to link the structure and organisation of communities of people to interactions with their local environment (Fontana Dictionary of Modern Thought).

Sustainable development is an open-ended concept. Not only is it open in the sense that the consequences of actions in terms of their effect on sustainability are not always clear, and may never be clear, in the last analysis. It is difficult to say what will or will not contribute to, or harm the chances of, sustainability in the long run.

An analogy of a 'lighthouse and the torch' has been used to describe the dilemma of sustainable development. On one hand there is a lighthouse, a beacon illuminating the vision in the unknown distance of the goal of sustainability. On the other hand, not only do we not know how far away the lighthouse is, but also we do not know what the terrain is between where we are now and where the lighthouse is. The way is dark and all we have is a small torch that allows us to see the terrain immediately around us, but nowhere near as far as is the lighthouse.

2.3 Applying the sustainable development concept to parts of the 'system'

Sustainable development and sustainability are concepts normally applied in the broadest sense to the future of the human race on Earth. However, short of world government taking actions that are widely regarded as legitimate, or pressure groups having the degree of legitimacy needed to get all or at least most people to behave in new ways, it is likely that progress towards general sustainability will require groupings of people and institutions to develop sustainable development practice for themselves and those immediately around them.   There are many activists in the sustainable development 'movement' that have focused on subsets of the human race and human activities. For example, at the Rio Earth Summit of 1991 great publicity was given not only to the broad concept of sustainable development for the Earth, but also to the view that local communities could make a difference to sustainability. This latter view became embodied in Agenda 21; various actions to promote sustainability in the 21st Century. Local communities, including local governments and local businesses as well as voluntary groups, have become an integral part of Agenda 21. Initiatives at this level are generally referred to as Local Agenda 21 (LA21). In addition many have developed policies in an attempt to encourage private companies and sub-sets of private companies, such as SMEs (Small and Medium Sized Enterprises) to embrace the concept of sustainable development, primarily by supporting policies to reduce their environmental impact and to show that such policies need not harm their financial position (Vetter, 1998; WWF, 1998).

The concept of sustainable development has been extended not only beyond a focus on the human race on Earth towards subsets of people and institutions as the action targets which will need to alter their actions in order to achieve sustainability of the world ecological system, but also towards those subsets of people and institutions as the aim of sustainable development: towards the sustainability of those people and institutions themselves, in certain aspects of their current form. In some ways the appeal of sustainable development to particular groups of people or institutions is that it holds out the possibility of increasing the chances of the sustainability of those groups. SMEs for example, are appealed to not only to get them to reduce their environmental impact, but also to 'do well out of doing good', by cutting costs of waste and improving their image or reputation in order to recruit young people or to win contracts with like minded organisations, by taking broader principles of sustainable development seriously and being seen to do so. It is not so far a leap to then apply the principles of sustainable development to individual organisations, to consider their sustainability by applying principles that have been developed for the sustainable development of the human race on Earth.

The value of applying the concepts of sustainable development and sustainability to groups of people and/or institutions is likely to vary with the complexity of those groups. More complex institutions with more complex links to wider environmental, economic and social systems are more likely to benefit from consideration of these concepts.

Clearly the professional associations sector, like other major sub-sets of the world ecological system such as local communities and SMEs, can make a difference in terms of sustainability of human life on this planet. However individually, professional associations are also complex institutions. Here we argue that the principles of sustainable development and sustainability can usefully be applied to professional associations individually as well as to them as a sector in their own right (see Chapter 3) or as part of the professional services sector. Here we consider the sustainability of professional associations as viable organisations and in so doing their sustainability also in terms of what they collectively stand for, the sustainability of their integrity as representatives of their members as professionals and their field of expertise as a profession as well as sustainability of the broad notion of a profession and its influence on human life on Earth.

2.4 Structural analysis of professional association complexity and their sustainable development

The lighthouse-torch analogy from Section 2.2, can help us to see that the sustainable development path is likely to always require careful steps and continual waving of the torch. What follows here and in the remaining sections of this chapter are not, and could not be, a definitive analysis and guide for the sustainable development of professional associations and the professional associations sector. Rather it is an analysis of the immediate terrain in which professional associations are currently situated, and an attempt at illuminating principles that can help to guide the next steps professional associations can take towards their sustainable development and that of the professions.

2.4.1 Overall complexity of aims of professional associations

We can take at least four different views of what is required for the sustainability of professional associations. These relate to four different spheres of activity based on different goals that may be espoused by or attributed to professional associations. These are goals toward: maintaining organisational integrity, the welfare and integrity of their members as professionals, the profession, and increasingly, the vitality of their 'sector', that is, professionalism in general. The first and last of these are bound up with particular ways of serving the public good. In effect we are saying that professional associations, like other third sector or non-profit organisations, have multiple bottom lines (Drucker, 1990) and may be viewed as conglomerates of organisations or of distinct component parts (Anheier, 2000). Non-profit organisations tend to be more complex than business firms of comparable size or they adhere to what Anheier calls the 'law of non-profit complexity'. However the manner in which professional associations are complex is different from most other non-profit organisations, different from public sector bodies and from distributing charities in particular, but also different from pure trade associations.

Professional association goals and roles are not only complex, but also conflicting, changing and uncertain. There is the conflict between the role many professional associations must play as advocates for the profession and their members, and the requirement that they perform a social good by regulating their members. Even when there are separate regulatory bodies such as the General Medical Council or the new Solicitors' Regulation Authority, the relevant professional bodies (Royal Medical Colleges and the British Medical Association, or the Law Society) are still expected by the general public to encourage members to be technically and ethically competent. Also there is the distinction between commitment to developing individual professional practitioners and developing the knowledge base, that is, the field of practice. The latter requires strong links with academics, while in many fields there are tensions between the interests of academics specialising on the knowledge base of a particular profession and the working practitioners. Even among practitioners the needs of different segments of the membership may conflict; such as the needs of members who offer a service directly to clients, either working on their own or in professional services firms, compared with those who work in other types of organisations. Their relations with government are overtly political and complex as they chart a course between acting as advisers and supplicants, and another complication is between performing a lobbying role and acting as *'lesser governments'* (MacDonald, 1995), regulating professional conduct and standards to protect society.

Professions are also in a state of flux (Friedman and Mason, 2004a; 2004b). The nature of the advocacy required and the services expected of them from their members are changing. Different goals and roles are challenged more specifically by members, government and the media at different times. Higher education institutions have been challenged to become more self-sufficient in their funding and this may be leading to a widening rift among academics in their loyalty towards their relevant professional bodies compared with the increasingly comprehensive and insistent demands of their higher education institutions. Employer attitudes are also changing, becoming less generous towards allowing staff time for involvement in governance, management and operations of professional bodies. These factors must be considered alongside changes in priorities among members; such as their growing concern for the 'value proposition' represented by membership fees; or their growing acceptance and expectations of CPD programmes, particularly that they be meaningfully linked to professional careers.

Another way of thinking about the added complexity of non-profit organisations is that in addition to finding the right mix of products (through effective planning) and producing those products efficiently (controlling costs), non-profits need to manage their stakeholder relations, which is a political process (Shoichet, 1998). While stakeholder management has been widely recommended as a strategic activity that private companies ought to engage in (Freeman, 1984), and there is considerable evidence that companies have been moving towards stakeholder management (Friedman and Miles, 2006), it is still widely regarded as aspirational and many would argue that stakeholder management is primarily cosmetic (see Friedman and Miles, 2006: Chapter 6). However, because of what might be called an 'accountability environment' that characterises non-profits, as emphasised by the Charity Commission in the UK, stakeholder management for them is substantially more important. This environment can include aspects of compliance, advocacy and negotiation within the relationship between the organisation and certain key stakeholders. For professional associations the key stakeholder group is current members (see Chapters 6 and 7 below), but others are also important, such as: potential members, clients of members, employers of members, government, the media, related professions and professional bodies, potential members.

2.4.2   Four 'bottom lines' for professional associations

The four different views of what is required for the sustainability and sustainable development of professional associations may be elaborated as follows:

1.   The sustainability (reliable viability) of themselves as organisations

- Maintaining adequate reserves and a healthy cash flow

- Diversifying income streams

- Instituting robust risk assessment and risk management systems

- Developing a strategic approach towards the running of the organisation

2. *The (material and status) interests of their members*

- Contributing to the material interests of members through:

  - o valuable services that improve personal wealth and/or the quality of the service that members can provide to their clients and/or employers

  - o services that improve the chances of members progressing by gaining new clients or improving their career prospects with employers

- Contributing to the status of members through:

  - o raising the position of the profession within the broader community

3. *The reputation (status and prestige) of their profession through sustaining and developing:*

- The knowledge base connected with their profession; the knowledge and techniques associated with their field of practice

- The competence of their members in that field of practice and this includes ethical and technical competence

- Advocacy for the profession with employers and government and maintaining a presence in the media

4. *The reputation (status and prestige) of professionalism as a concept*

- Ensuring that the public and government is aware of the importance of professionalism

- Being certain of the activities under 1 and 2 above, however not at the expense of other professional groups

- This may embrace joint activities among professional associations across sectors

- This may be thought of as the equivalent of the environment in which professional associations operate, whether it is benign or antagonistic to the general mission of professional associations

These four areas are related, but different from each other. Certain activities and policies will further several of these aims, and some will indeed further all of them, such as, for example, a well-developed and effective CPD policy and programme. However, other activities which further one of the aims, are likely to either have no effect on furthering the other aims, or may actually put them at risk. For example, the Charity Commission explicitly forbids (see Charity Commission, 2003) organisations with charitable status from including in their objects the aim of furthering the material interests of members of those organisations.

One way of representing these four different bottom lines of professional associations is to think of them as concerned with different 'environments' that surround the professional association as an organisation. This is represented in Figure 2:1.

Figure 2:1   Professional associations and their sustainability

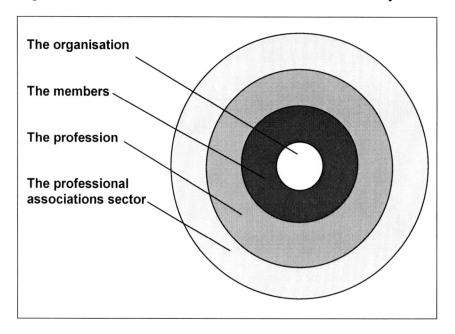

The organisation

The members

The profession

The professional associations sector

Professional associations are organisations, which must maintain financial, organisational and reputational integrity in order to survive and develop: integrity in this case meaning being true to purpose and reliably viable. Professional associations must, like private sector organisations, maintain a positive cash flow, or at least have built up substantial reserves in order to carry the organisation over periods of inadequate cash flow. This is a perspective on professional associations that is not widely discussed in academic circles. The sociologists have been primarily concerned with the professions and individual professionals; how they interact with clients and what are the implications of the rise of the professions for the stability and morality of developed societies. Management academics are mainly interested in private companies and therefore in the professional services firms. Even those few that are interested in the 'third sector' are primarily concerned with distributing charities. Academics in the areas that are the subject fields of the professions are generally limited in their scope to their particular professional field. To some extent management and business knowledge generated in relation to private companies also apply to professional associations. However, as noted above, professional associations are more complex.

Secondly, and most obviously to those that manage professional associations, these organisations have been formed, by and large, by groups of professionals. Members and their interests must be important to professional associations. While it is sometimes not clear from the objects of professional associations that they serve their members, it is difficult to avoid member interests, concerns, needs and wishes when the governing body is largely elected from the members, as is still most common. Certain member interests coincide with other of the bottom lines of professional associations, but some do not and can conflict. This sometimes comes to a head when associations come to raise subscription rates.

Professional associations are most obviously concerned with their respective and individual professions, with promoting the standing of the profession through maintaining standards of practice and encouraging the best to apply to join the profession. This is in line with the common sociological interpretations of the professions, that is, that they are characterised by professional upward social mobility projects (Larson, 1977) and jurisdictional competition (Abbott, 1988). The interconnected nature of different professional associations is characterised by competition among professional groups. This impacts on professional groups as one of them expands into the jurisdiction of another or as technological changes lead to work normally carried out by people with certain expertise, now being carried out by others. Sustainability of one professional group can depend on successfully fending off others or developing cooperative relations with them. Nevertheless, raising the standing of one profession need not require denigrating others. Most professions are battling not with other professions, but rather with scepticism from potential clients as to the knowledge base and appropriateness of the techniques being offered by particular professions as well as their trustworthiness, that is, their technical and ethical competence at delivering the particular professional service they offer.

Less obviously, but just as important, professional associations must be concerned with the wider environment in which they operate, not only the natural environment, but also the wider social environment, that is the ecology of professional associations as a population and the state of professionalism as a concept in this country and the world as a whole. Here the damage that one profession does to itself reflects badly on all professions. All professions have been affected by Enron and the collapse of accountants Arthur Anderson. All professions have been affected, at least in the UK, by Harold Shipman's murders and by the perceived ineffectiveness of the medical profession and the General Medical Council in particular, to have taken action against Shipman long before he eventually came to trial. The effect of media attention on professional misdeeds can be felt across the professions; the falling off of trust (at least blind trust) in many, the rise in law suits against professionals, the demand for professionals to demonstrate that they are keeping up to date, even to the point of CPD affecting premiums on professional indemnity insurance. These are all aspects of the importance of the standing of professionalism per se, for the sustainability of individual professional associations. In some ways this is even more important for the professional associations that are strongest, whose professionalism is least questioned, because their strength is based on the foundation of professionalism itself being of recognised value.

The three rings around the organisation depicted in Figure 2:1 should not be thought of as completely distinct and the order in which they appear invariant. As noted above, policies aimed at improving one of these bottom lines can affect the others as well. The order of the rings is intended to suggest which aims are closest to the organisation. We regard the positioning of the rings to be more relevant to pure professional associations, however this is debatable and aims for the profession is certainly more likely to be the closest for learned societies. Also we could suggest another bottom line; the contribution to the public good. However this is implied by the aims towards the profession and the professional associations sector. It is through this that professional associations aim, and are expected to aim, to serve the public good.

2.4.3   Complexity in the structure of professional associations

Professional associations are complicated, not only in terms of their multiple bottom lines, but also in the lack of control they have over their surroundings and even their own activities. This is because they rely to some extent on voluntary effort, and some rely on it entirely (see Chapter 4 Section 4.2.2). They do not have the level of control that organisations which only rely on paid staff have. This is the opposite side of the characteristic of professional associations' need to consider the political process of managing stakeholder relations. Managing stakeholder relations, especially member relations, cannot be done without a much greater degree of consent that would be required of employees. Professional associations are particularly 'networked organisations' due to their club-like nature. They must support and maintain an informal 'college' or community of practice, largely relying on the consent of the membership. They need to keep members involved in the field of practice, the techniques of practice, as well as the more theoretical aspects of the knowledge base through their journals and newsletters and their CPD programmes and they must encourage sharing of good practice techniques through face-to-face networking activities such as are generated through branch and special interest group structures. This is different from almost all other organisations. It also introduces a further element of uncertainty to how professional associations operate.

2.5 Strategies and processes for achieving sustainable development of professional associations

2.5.1 Introduction

Here we consider three broad types of strategies that can be applied by professional associations in order to support their sustainable development. These, to some extent, mirror the general principles derived from the sustainable development literature in Section 2.2 above.

First, and most obviously important for dealing with sustainability, is *risk assessment and risk management*. This strategy for supporting sustainability is widely known with a well-established market of consultants and trainers offering to support organisations. It is essential to follow-up risk assessment exercises with risk management techniques. Some of these techniques are simple and relatively cheap, such as insurance, others can involve major organisation changes, such as ceasing certain lines of activity and/or pursuing new lines.

A second, and less well-explored method of achieving sustainable development is to carry out policies that at once answer at least more than one of the *multiple goals* of the organisation. This represents what may be called externalities; reflecting the adage of 'killing two birds with one stone'. Pursuing one activity, such as updating the association's ethical code, can lead to unexpected benefits for member relations by encouraging focused trainers to develop CPD on the new code. This is likely to require those taking the course to work through examples of ethical dilemmas in groups. Such courses extend the range of CPD offered by the association and may encourage members to take a more positive attitude towards their CPD obligations, as they are offered a course which is directly relevant to their work and one which would be difficult to carry out through personal study alone.

A third method is to build for the future by carrying out activities that will lead, in time, to the emergence of further positive activities or for existing ones to become more effective. This represents what may be called 'time-dependent ecological effects'. Taking the above example of revising the ethical code: The revised code may not only lead to members and potential members of the profession being clearer about what obligations are expected of them, it may also lead to the association making the code more accessible to the general public, initially simply to inform the general public of what the association is doing. However, in doing this the association can be led to consider the importance of accessibility of the code to both members and the general public. It may lead the association to provide better support for the code in terms of education and training as well as sharpening complaints and disciplinary procedures. The example of CPD courses developing around the new code is also likely to take time to emerge.

Using the concept of sustainability to frame the activities described here can be helpful if it encourages those governing and managing associations to think through the connections and to take a strategic or a professional stance towards them. It is possible that carrying out a risk assessment exercise will by itself sensitise staff to major risks and encourage more care; it is possible that certain actions intended to achieve one of the goals of the association will 'automatically' lead to progress towards other goals; it may be that the time-dependent ecological effects will 'naturally' emerge. Certainly we do believe that this sometimes occurs. Updating the ethical code is one of those sorts of activities that are likely to lead to both 'instant' external economies and time-dependent ecological effects. One of the purposes of this chapter is to encourage associations to pursue activities that are more likely to generate these multi-goal and time-enhancing effects.

Another purpose of this chapter is to emphasise that these sustainability-enhancing features will not occur with certainty. There is dark space between the lighthouse and the torch. However, it seems obvious that such sustainability-enhancing features are more likely to occur if the activities are done well. Even activities that are most likely 'naturally' to yield these sustainability-enhancing effects must be carried out with care and with sufficient resources. Updating an ethical code badly, without regard to member views, without regard to current practice in other professions where this exercise has recently been carried out, without regard to the latest thinking issued by the Charity Commission and the Better Regulation Commission,[6] can lead to an exercise and a new code that is not regarded as useful or even legitimate by members and the general public. Carrying out a survey of members, for example, can be worse than useless, can actually reduce member satisfaction with the association, if member opinions do not result in what they regard as satisfactory action. Several executives of

---

[6] Dare we say without reading recent PARN books on the subject?

associations recognise this and it is one reason for not carrying out such surveys, because they do not want to build unrealisable expectations among members. Nevertheless, even the delivery of actual services can reduce member satisfaction, rather than increase it, if the service is considered inappropriate, shoddy or delivered in an insensitive manner.

Following on from understanding the particular importance of pursuing sustainability-enhancing *activities* well, is the value of taking a strategic or reflective approach to the sustainability enhancing *processes* that we describe below. Not only are these positive effects unlikely to occur if the activity itself is carried out badly, but also they are more likely to occur, and occur in ways more likely to improve sustainability, if they are consciously pursued.

Here professionalisation and sustainability of professional associations become fused. The revised ethical code may be clearer and more up-to-date. The group tasked with revising the code may do a good job, and the aim of clarifying obligations owed by members may be well done. However, the other aim of the association, to reassure the public, may not be achieved if the promulgation of the code is not thought out. At PARN we recommend that codes should be accessible on association websites by members of the public. More than this, we recommend that the code should be easily accessible from the association's homepage, preferably within one or two clicks (see Friedman et al. 2005). Similarly a CPD course connected to the new ethical code may emerge from the market, but it can also be commissioned by the association, and timed to coincide with the delivery of the new code.

2.5.2 Risk management methods of improving sustainability

Certain actions can be taken either to reduce the likelihood of disasters occurring (precautionary actions) or lessen their impact when they do occur (alleviative actions). Closely related to the latter are actions to manage and monitor situations that can deteriorate.

Precautionary actions
Three kinds of precautionary actions are:

- Avoidance actions, that is, after due assessment, deciding that certain activities involve too high a risk to tolerate and there is no other way to deal with this risk

- Prophylactic action - taking safety precautions; that is, protecting operations with a barrier or a 'cordone sanitaire', instituting what may be regarded as hygiene factors. Analogous to applying DEET if one is going to the tropics or taking malaria pills. Some organisations literally achieve this by hiring security guards. Security systems to block access to sensitive IT systems and data are another example.

- Anticipating specific disasters that might occur as a result of human error or from benign or even encouraging environmental factors turning into malevolent ones. This may involve actions such as keeping informed of government intentions based on searching for such information or by maintaining a presence on committees that advise government. Similarly developing intelligence about member needs and desires as well as their views on the services they receive, and taking action based on this information, can reduce the chances of losing members.

Alleviative actions
These involve taking actions that will either reduce the degree to which sustainability may be threatened by activities or actions that cannot be controlled. They include:

- spreading risks through diversifying income sources

- insuring against risk through back-up facilities or taking advantage of a wide variety of insurance schemes.

Management and monitoring activities
There are many ways to manage and monitor risks. Two different approaches are:

- give managers of processes specific remits to deal with adverse events as they arise, for example, dealing with member complaints and requests

- assign specific individuals other than process managers to monitor risk and deal with adverse events, in addition to their normal duties.

These policies are not costless. Alternative income streams and the reduction in the impact of any one stream faltering, must be weighed against the costs of developing alternative income streams. It must also take into account the possibility that these alternative income streams may dilute the professional image of the association and the trust others have in how seriously the association takes its aims of keeping up the reputation of the profession and the reputation of professionalism in general.

2.5.3   Multiple goal methods of sustainable development

There are some policies that can serve several of the association's goals at the same time. An example is the development of a CPD policy and programme in the current climate. This will increase the prestige of the profession by helping to ensure that members are up to date and by increasing the prestige of the professions as a whole, by ensuring that standards are being maintained beyond initial professional qualifications. It can also lead to income streams and, perhaps more important, contribute to the status and prestige of individual members, particularly as CPD becomes part of the requirement for achieving fellowship or other higher grade status in the profession. It also helps to signal to the public that fellowship is not merely an honorific title in the profession.

Another example, of a more limited nature, is the development and regular review of a professional ethical code and policies to encourage members to take the code seriously. This serves the profession and professionalism in general as well as raising the prestige of individual members.

CPD and ethics policies are generally what may be regarded as *super-activities* by professional associations. There are other activities that are likely to be super-activities in terms of serving multiple goals, such as getting a Royal Charter and developing critical qualifications. Not only do they cross different aims of the profession, they also complement those aims, one with the other, and this can lead to long-term effects described in the next section. As noted in Section 2.5.1, it is important for those managing professional associations to recognise the significance of these super-activities both to be sure that they are carried out well, and to take a strategic approach to policies and activities that can stimulate and develop the links that may naturally occur towards multiple goal achievement.

2.5.4 Connecting methods that operate over time in order to secure sustainable development

Taking a strategic approach to activities with strong time-dependent ecological effects is also important. Not all activities carried out by professional associations have strong time-dependent ecological effects. The key distinguishing factor is activities that have an effect on their environment meaning primarily the ecology in which associations and the whole professional associations sector is situated (but also meaning the natural environment). We attempt to classify activities based on this characteristic below.

2.5.4.1 Some activities have little 'ecological' effect

Some activities have little effect on wider environments or ecologies. They may be too small in themselves, or they may not do more than reproduce the current situation. Many member services in the form of affinity deals fall into this category. It is not that they cannot be of value to members, but rather that they do not change the position of associations compared to each other or the sector compared to other sectors, largely because these kinds of deals can be had elsewhere. Provision of other expected services such as member newsletters can also fall into this category. There are also many formal management control techniques, which may have an effect on service delivery or on efficiency of the association, but in themselves may have little effect on the association's environment, such as setting up regular internal team meetings and management information systems.

In general, the way an association develops activities and the timing of those activities in the context of the wider ecology of professional associations can be just as important for its ecological effect as the activity itself. An association that follows others in taking on new services, or even a new way of professionalising itself (such as introducing risk management systems), but in a manner which is little different from what is already being done by others, may have little effect on its environment one way or another, and may only contribute to its goals in the sense of avoiding reduced success or even failure at these goals if it had not acted. On the other hand, an association that is an early adopter of such techniques, or one that makes that adoption a feature of its publicity and the subject of careful reflection, can have a substantial positive effect on its goals and on its stakeholders. This may lead to further positive views of the association among other stakeholders who are not directly affected by the policy, and this may ultimately rebound positively back to the association, say by improving the number and quality of recruits to the profession.

2.5.4.2 *Some activities have only effects in one sphere over time as well as immediately*

As noted in the previous section, some activities have multiple effects on association aims, some do not. Ones that do not have an immediate spill-over effect may eventually affect more than one of the goals or stakeholders of an association. For example, a policy to reduce costs in the association by outsourcing certain functions may lead to an improvement in member interests if the money is used to keep member subscription fees low. This policy is not likely to have effects on other goals or other stakeholders of the association either immediately or in the long run. This is not to say that it is not a good policy to pursue in certain circumstances, only that its effects are limited on the sustainability of the association (unless the association is in the midst of a financial crisis or a crisis of member retention). On the other hand, a policy to outsource IT functions could have a long term effect, not only on costs, but also on the profession in the context of other professional associations, if it is done in conjunction with another profession or with a group of professions, say through an umbrella group such as the Engineering Council or the Construction Industry Council, as it may then strengthen those organisations which may, in turn, have an effect on the standing of those professions.

2.5.4.3 *Some activities have substantial ecological effects over time and in multiple spheres*

Creating and amplifying positive effects

Some activities take time to have an effect on the ecology of associations, others have an almost immediate effect. The Enron affair had rapid and significant implications. It led to the collapse of Arthur Anderson, one of the top accounting firms in the world. It also led to the rapid, some would say hasty, passing of the Sarbanes-Oxley Act in the US. It led to innumerable reports and clear damage to the accounting profession as well as to professionalism in general, all within a few short years.

On the other hand, substantial efforts over the past 20 years among professional associations to 'professionalise themselves' have gone largely unnoticed, even, in some instances, among the membership of those professional associations. However, we believe that these activities will eventually pay off, not merely with increased member satisfaction and organisational sustainability, but also through raising the status of those professions that vigorously embrace this set of activities, and the philosophy or culture behind it, as well as contributing to a growing appreciation of the importance of professionalism in society.

Here are some examples of principles that may lead policies or programmes to have a high chance of affecting the ecology of the association and thereby having substantial interconnecting effects over time:

- Pioneer policies or activities

- Well-publicised activities, preferably ones that lead to long-term media interest

- Activities that become standards (possibly through formal regulatory action)

- Activities that lead to changes in the legal framework within which associations operate.

The process we are concerned with here is:

- First, what effect does an action of the association have immediately on the fortunes of the association?

- Second, what is the amplification (and diminution) of this effect following from a change in activities undertaken by professional associations as a result of changing the landscape of activities, interests and attitudes which are connected parts of the ecology of associations; that is, actions, interests and attitudes of stakeholders of the association?

- Third, whether these secondary effects lead to further reactions within the association in the same or opposite direction, and further amplified or diminished? For example, it may be that the first associations to introduce serious CPD programmes have had an effect on the overall attitude towards CPD among professionals. This then may push early adopters of CPD to upgrade their programmes. What may have begun as an experiment eventually becomes core to the reputation and identity of the pioneer association.

Diminution of positive effects
Positive time-dependent ecological effects emerge from certain activities naturally, but are not always guaranteed to occur and their strength can diminish. For some activities there may be a cycle of positive effects. Revising a code may improve an association's reputation with the general public in the short run, but this positive effect may fall off in time as the new code no longer seems new. The value of a professional association's technical journal or set of technical journals can diminish because its very success has stimulated competition from journals of other associations or independent groups of academics, particularly if the professional association does not keep abreast of latest developments in the field and adds new journals to its offering. This is a common occurrence, particularly as continually rising pressures to publish among academics connected to the profession lead them to both support new journals by submitting manuscripts for consideration as well as to develop new journals and build reputation through editorships.

Creating and amplifying negative effects
Scandals based on major lapses of technical and/or ethical competence are the clearest cases of negative ecological effects. Particularly if:

- The harm done to what are regarded as ordinary members of the public is great, such as medical professionals responsible for death or major disablement

- Many in the general public are affected, such as for cases of pension or insurance mis-selling involving many clients

- The professional association can be regarded as at fault in some manner, usually by not picking up on the lapses early enough or being viewed as too lax on those who have directly lapsed or who are responsible for misdeeds; such as the Shipman case or past concerns about how long it takes for complaints about lawyers to be dealt with

- A view by the general public that a high proportion of particular professions are lapsing in some way, such as the view that the length of time taken to deal with complaints against lawyers reflects the large number of lawyers complained about

- If the specific lapse of standards of ethics can be generalised as crossing traditional professional sector boundaries.

Obviously these situations are essential to avoid and this is a major reason for carrying out risk analysis and risk management. In those analyses it is important to recognise the full consequences of hazards occurring. That is, long term as well as short term consequences, even if long term consequences are much harder to quantify.

- Chapter 3 -
Professional associations as a distinguishable 'sector'

3.1 The 'sector' of professional associations: two views

It is a 'natural' consequence of the establishment of PARN that we should come to think of professional associations as a sector and that we should encourage people governing and managing those organisations to consider themselves as operating in this context. PARN is dedicated to the idea that professional associations share enough common concerns, are subject to sufficient common pressures and wish to achieve aims that are sufficiently similar (both complementary and in some instances competing) to the extent that nearly all can benefit from research about the sector and from networking among themselves in the context of reflecting on this research. However, it is not clear precisely how to draw the line around professional associations to support the standpoint that they are a sector. What distinguishes this set of organisations as a sector? Here we offer two perspectives on how the line may be drawn around professional associations to distinguish them as a sector. We believe that both are 'interesting' in that sensitivity to them can increase both the value of research and networking among professional associations and can also help them to see a wider value of further interaction among themselves.

3.1.1 An essential adjunct to the professional services sector

Professional associations organise the 'production' of professionals and the maintenance of practitioners as professionals (though not alone). They also support (represent, promote and secure standards and development of) the knowledge base, the practice and the standing and influence of certain fields of knowledge associated with particular occupations[7].

If we consider the traditional sector division from the perspective of the censuses of economic activity, professional associations are part of the tertiary or services sector. This sector is also traditionally divided into sectors or sub-sectors, such as retail services, financial services, legal services, medical services. However it is not uncommon to distinguish professional services within the tertiary sector (see for example Greenwood et al., 2002).

Professional services are inherently different from other goods and services. They do not have a fixed specification that can be easily judged. Clients of professionals often do not, and cannot, know precisely what services they require until advised by the professional. Professionals will generally know more than clients about the quality and value of the service the professionals provide before it is provided, while it is provided and after the provision is complete. There will always be 'information asymmetries' between professional 'suppliers' and client or patient 'consumers' of professionals. This makes those receiving services from professionals and those commissioning or directing them vulnerable. It is difficult to know who is a competent and ethical professional to choose to hire (the well known problem of 'adverse selection' in economics; see Fama and Jensen, 1983). Furthermore it will also be difficult to know whether the professional taken on is doing or has done a good job (so-called 'moral hazard' in economics). Clearly the severity of these problems varies considerably among professions. However the existence of these problems underpins the professional status of any occupational group.

These information asymmetries also exist for managers hiring and directing professionals employed in organisations that are not direct providers of professional services. Primary and secondary sector organisations directly employ professionals in many capacities as do public sector organisations and professional services firms providing services other than those which are delivered to them by professional employees. Professionals supported by certain professional bodies even provide services and are employed by other professional bodies. In all these situations inherent information asymmetries still exist

---

[7] We use the term professional associations here, but include regulatory bodies, learned societies and awarding bodies.

between those hiring and managing professionals and the professionals themselves.

Professional associations are essential for professional services in their role as suppliers of qualified practitioners to professional services firms and in maintaining their professionalism. In a sense, professional services firms trade on the basis of an externality provided by professional associations. This is recognised by many large professional services firms when they pay the subscription fees for their employees to the relevant professional association.

Professional associations may be thought of as occupying a section of the supply chain by which certain inputs are designed, produced and delivered which are essential for professional services firms to operate. The essential input that the professional associations sector 'produces' for professional services firms is 'qualified' practitioners. There are a number of components to this 'product'. These include:

- The design of initial professional qualifications and the setting of standards for these qualifications

- Delivery and examination of education (theoretical, technical, ethical) and other (experience-based) qualifications

- Design and setting standards for CPD

- Delivery and examination of CPD

- Design and promulgation of ethical codes

- Positive support for ethical codes, mainly in the form of education and training involved in 1 and 3 above

- Support for dealing with professional misconduct through complaints and disciplinary procedures.

These activities are all directly relevant to the individuals. In addition professional associations provide, along with certain (primarily higher) education institutions, another set of inputs to the professional services sector. This is the development of the knowledge base that underlies a particular professional occupation. This combination of theory and practical techniques comprises a field of professional knowledge and is an essential input not only to professional services firms, but also to professional associations themselves. The role of professional associations in relation to the knowledge base is perhaps best thought of as a stewardship role. This can involve directly developing the knowledge base, though often this is carried out within education institutions. The knowledge base is also developed within practice and an important role of professional associations is to bring practitioners together around topics of practice and the development of new techniques of practice, in order to diffuse this knowledge as well as to further develop it. Professional associations also sponsor research and spread that knowledge through their journals and newsletters as well as conferences and workshops.

The professional services sector of the economy is unique in that it embraces two distinct components: professional services firms and professional associations. Arguably this is a peculiarly Anglophile construction. Strong and independent professional association components of the professional services sector are particularly strong in the UK and Ireland, but also in the United States, Canada and Australia, India and South Africa. On the other hand, on Continental Europe, professionalism is more closely tied to higher education institutions (such as the Grandes Ecoles in France), which are themselves more closely tied to State institutions.

3.1.2   A sub-sector of the 'third' sector

Another way of thinking of professional bodies is as a sector or sub-sector of the economy and society is in the manner in which they are constituted and their ultimate purpose. As such professional bodies are a collection of overwhelmingly 'third sector' organisations (sometimes labelled voluntary organisations or associations): 'between' private companies and the public sector. A few are public sector (some regulatory bodies for certain professions, such as the Health Professions Council, have been set up by the government and are funded by the government) and some professional associations have set up private for-profit commercial organisations to provide support for their public benefit activities more effectively. It is our impression that the proportion of the sector composed of these commercial organisations is growing, however the vast proportion of professional bodies are third sector organisations; that is, they are associations that are constituted as not-for-profit organisations and are not part of the public sector.

This third sector can be divided into five sub-sectors:

- distributing charities

- pressure groups or campaigning organisations

- trade associations

- trade unions

- professional bodies.

Most people when they think of the third sector think of charities. Indeed a fairly high proportion of all five sub-sectors identified here are actually formally constituted in the UK as charitable bodies and operate under regulations set by the Charity Commission. However this is not true for all of them and the proportion of professional associations constituted as charities depends not only on their desire to work for the public benefit, but also on certain features of charities law, such as the ease with which the Charity Commission grants charitable status to organisations and the tax advantages (and disadvantages) of having charitable status. A few professional bodies embrace distributing charities, these are generally benevolent funds for members of the profession who have fallen on hard times. The benevolent fund is formulated as a separate organisation with its own trustees.

There are other overlaps within the sector. For example some professional bodies are also trade unions, perhaps the most well known is the British Medical Association. Trade unions are distinguished by their function of negotiating on behalf of their members with employers over pay and conditions and for defending their members in relation to grievances in the workplace. Some professional bodies carry out such functions for their professional members who are employees. However professional bodies that are trade unions carry out professional functions as well, that is, they support ethical and technical standards of practice and help to further the knowledge base of the occupation.

Some professional associations are also trade associations, or carry out the functions of trade associations. This may be expected when the members of a professional association are both professionals and proprietors of their own professional services firms or are partners in a professional services firm. However these days many professionals in practice work in organisations in which relatively few are partners or owners. Some professional associations also have members that are professional services firms that are not sole traderships or partnerships. However the proportion of professional association members that are companies is generally low. In the 2006 survey it was just under 3% (based on 96 cases) in the UK and 7% in Ireland (based on 19 cases). Many that have company members do not define themselves as trade associations, for example, 90% of those in the UK with corporate members did not identify themselves as trade associations in addition to professional associations (see Chapter 6 Section 6.2 for further details).

Some professional associations take on the function of pressure groups as well in relation to particular government policies. In fact most professional associations may be regarded as pressure groups in broad support of the knowledge field behind the professional practice of their members. In this sense many professional bodies would consider themselves to be learned societies. A few, such as the medical Royal Colleges, consider themselves to be exclusively learned societies. Many are a combination of professional association and learned society where the learned society aspect is older and more significant in terms of the activities of the society.

3.2   Survey results on 'defining' functions carried out by professional bodies

Professional bodies can take on a variety of functions as noted above. In addition to being professional associations, concerned with standards of their members and the reputation of the subject, they could also be trade unions, trade associations or learned societies. One further function associations can take on, which supports their role as providers of suitable professional practitioners, is as providers of evidence of education and training, or 'awards'. Most accredit the education and training provision of others, but some carry out the examinations themselves and some are directly involved in the education and training provision.

One important distinction is between professional associations and regulatory bodies. The traditional professions were distinguished as being self-regulating. They therefore carried out two different functions. They were concerned with the interests of their members and with disciplining their members. Some may consider these to be incompatible functions. However if the overwhelming proportion of professionals are motivated by altruism, and there are only a few who either do not understand the requirements or are 'bad apples', then the two functions need not be incompatible in a single organisation, as long as there are robust processes and a clear separation in the management of each. However self-regulation is under threat. In the last few years a number of recommendations have been made for associations to devolve these functions to other agencies and the government has set up independent regulatory bodies for certain professions, perhaps the most prominent of these is the new Solicitors Regulation Authority which has been separated out from the Law Society of England and Wales.

In the 2006 PARN Professionalisation Survey, respondents were asked what type of organisation they were and asked to tick all of those specified in Table 3:1 that applied to them. All but 2 from the UK responded to this question.

Table 3:1   Types of organisation in the UK and Ireland

Type of organisation	% responding UK[1]	% responding Ireland[1]	% responding to this category *alone* in UK[2]	% responding to this category *alone* in Ireland[2]
Professional association	93%	100%	51%	71%
Learned society	24%	5%	3%	0
Trade union	12%	10%	0	0
Regulatory body	9%	14%	1%	0
Awarding body[3]	7%	n/a	1%	n/a
Trade association	7%	10%	3%	0

[1] Adds up to more than 100% as respondents selected more than one option.

[2] Adds up to less than 100% as excludes respondents that selected more than one option.

[3] Note that the option of 'awarding body' was not offered in the Irish survey.

Roughly half of respondents in the UK classified their organisation as a professional association alone. In the UK, roughly a quarter of respondents classified their organisations as learned societies, but only 3% as learned societies alone[8]. This was very different in Ireland where only 5% classified their organisations as learned societies. Of those who ticked more than one category, the full set of combinations is shown in Table 3:2.

The most common combination in the UK was professional association and learned society, followed by professional association and trade union. A rather interesting case was the single one that was both a trade union and a trade association in addition to being a professional association. In Ireland the most common combinations were professional association and regulatory body, and professional association and trade association.

---

[8] One of these was a medical Royal College, however, the other two were an institution and a society with individual professionally qualified members. We show the answers to these options based on whatever was ticked by the respondents, though we would have interpreted the question as requiring those two bodies to tick both professional association and learned society.

Table 3:2   Combinations of types of organisation

Combination of types of organisations	% responding to the combination UK	% responding to the combination in Ireland
Professional association & learned society	15%	0
Professional association & trade union	9%	5%
Professional association & regulatory body	3%	10%
Professional association & awarding body	3%	n/a
Professional association & trade association	2%	10%
Professional association & learned society & regulatory body	4%	0
Professional association & learned society & trade union	2%	0
Professional association & learned society & awarding body	1%	n/a
Professional association & learned society & regulatory body & trade union	0	5%
Professional association & regulatory body & awarding body	2%	n/a
Professional association & trade union & trade association	1%	0
Total	42%	30%

Table 3:3 shows the changes in these categories by comparing the answers for the 60 UK professional bodies that answered this question in both the 2003 and 2006 surveys. We can only show crude changes because in 2003 the options 'trade association' and 'awarding body' were not offered. They were presumably included in 'other' in the minds of respondents in 2003.

Table 3:3 Changes in types of organisation in the UK: 2003 and 2006

Type of organisation	% responding 2003	% responding 2006	% responding to this category *alone* 2003	% responding to this category *alone* 2006
Professional association	97%	95%	50%	43%
Learned society	60%	60%	0	3%
Trade union	23%	27%	3%	0
Regulatory body	27%	27%	0	0
Other	10%	17%	0	2%

Table 3:3 indicates very little change in the sample between the two years.

3.3 Professional associations as distinctive organisations

While in the previous section we examined the range of functions which professional associations can take on and in so doing emphasised certain overlaps between them and other types of organisations as well as emphasising that the sector of professional associations is variegated with different bodies taking on a different range of functions, here we emphasise what is distinctive about them.

Professional associations are organisations, albeit different from private companies, public sector bodies and even other third sector organisations such as distributing charities or campaigning organisations. As organisations, professional associations must be concerned with their sustainability, if they are to continue to achieve the objectives set out in their foundation documents. However, they are special and at PARN we have been concerned to define, analyse and make recommendations based on what is special about professional associations as well as what they share with other organisations.

They are, like other third sector organisations, what may be called mission-driven[9], that is, they are generally not-for-profit organisations and are, guided by a set of principles or missions enshrined in a memorandum of association and in articles of association, which contain statements that are, for many, phrased as charitable objects to achieve public benefit in some way[10].

According to the Charity Commission website (Charity Commission, 2003):

> *52. The objects set out what a charity is set up to do. They should therefore be described clearly and unambiguously in the governing document, using words with a commonly accepted meaning. A charity may have more than one object.*

---

[9] We reserve the term mission-driven for associations not constituted as private limited-liability companies. However those that are may be called mission-oriented; that is, for them there is something that is more important than profit, though profit is one of the objects. The difference is that for mission-oriented firms profit can, at some time become the primary, even the exclusive focus, without contradicting their prime objects. This frequently happens when the culture of the company changes in consequence of a strong leader or the founding entrepreneur, who had been guiding the company according to her or his mission, leaves the company or relinquishes control to others, often through a takeover, as for example when Ben and Jerry's was taken over by Unilever in 2001 (Friedman and Miles, 2006: 254).

[10] According to the Charity Commission website *'52. The objects set out what a charity is set up to do. They should therefore be described clearly and unambiguously in the governing document, using words with a commonly accepted meaning. A charity may have more than one object. 53. It is important to remember that: all of the objects must be charitable, because if any aspect of them is not, the organisation cannot be accepted as a charity because it will not be exclusively charitable; the objects should reflect what the organisation intends to do; and the objects should be understandable'.* (Charity Commission, 2003) In addition they state that *'the memorandum of association of every company must state the objects of the company: usually the objects of a company are set out in the objects clause. Modern drafting practice in the case of charitable companies is to exclude from the objects clause any provision which is not strictly speaking an object of the company. But, particularly in the case of older companies, the objects clause may include not only the objects of the company but also the powers to be used by the company in furthering those objects. ... amendment of any provision in the objects clause requires our prior written consent under Section 64(2)(a), whether or not it is, strictly speaking, an "object".'*

53. It is important to remember that: all of the objects must be charitable, because if any aspect of them is not, the organisation cannot be accepted as a charity because it will not be exclusively charitable; the objects should reflect what the organisation intends to do; and the objects should be understandable.

They also state that:

... the memorandum of association of every company must state the objects of the company: usually the objects of a company are set out in the objects clause. Modern drafting practice in the case of charitable companies is to exclude from the objects clause any provision which is not strictly speaking an object of the company. But, particularly in the case of older companies, the objects clause may include not only the objects of the company but also the powers to be used by the company in furthering those objects. ... amendment of any provision in the objects clause requires our prior written consent under Section 64(2)(a), whether or not it is, strictly speaking, an "object".

In addition many are Chartered bodies and these principles or the mission is enshrined in their Royal Charter. However, like all non-government bodies, professional associations must operate in a sustainable manner. They must maintain themselves as viable organisations financially and this requires certain activities to be performed that are the same as those required of for profit organisations. That is, they must ensure that their costs do not exceed their income over an extended period. In addition, as mission-driven organisations in most instances, they must ensure that they are adequately representing and furthering the aims and objectives set out in their governing documents. They must, for example, develop the field of knowledge and expertise associated with their profession. They must ensure that the profession is practiced to a minimum standard and act to raise that standard over time through encouraging technical progress in the field and the distribution of new techniques through initial professional training and continuing professional development. They must take measures to ensure that member practitioners are acting ethically, by producing ethical codes and supporting those codes either through encouragement by publicity and education concerning the code and its implications for ethical conduct, or in some instances, by disciplining those that do not comply with the code or who do not demonstrate adequate ethical and technical competence.

Unlike other third sector organisations such as distributing charities or campaigning organisations (NGOs), professional associations, are answerable to their membership. The relationship between the association and the membership is stronger and more emotionally charged than the relationship between private sector organisations and their shareholders or between distributing charities and their contributors. This is because members of professional bodies are at the same time:

- Often constituted as the owners of the association or at least those charged with the governance of the association

- Reliant on the association for their professional identity that is, for the maintenance of their livelihood and often the privileged position in the occupational hierarchy they occupy as well as for the basis of their status and prestige in the community

- The primary consumers of services produced by the association

- Many are also providers of voluntary services to the association.

Because of these various and intimate connections, professional associations must be sensitive to the interests of the membership. The association can serve the interests of the membership best not simply through providing them material benefits of membership, but primarily (and when constituted as a charity officially exclusively) through the provision of benefits that serve the public good through profession-enhancing activities that then bring credit to the membership. In addition the professional association must maintain the confidence of the profession as a whole (that is non-members who are still practitioners of the profession), the government (often particularly through the Charity Commission and the Privy Council which regulates Royal Charters, as well as a range of occupation specific government departments and regulatory bodies), and the general public (often as it is represented in the mass media) that the aims and objectives are being maintained. In this sense professional bodies have both multiple bottom lines and multiple critical stakeholders. They have a number of different aims and goals that cannot be summarised simply in terms of a single measure of success such as profit or long run shareholder value. They have a number of different stakeholder groups, whose goodwill is essential to the association, both directly, and indirectly through the effect of their goodwill on the status and material interests of the members. Adverse media attention, for example, can be directed directly to the professional body, and it can also be directed to the profession and its members. Effects on the latter can lead them to demand more of the association.

Another distinctive aspect of professional associations, though one shared by distributing charities, is that they rely to varying degrees on voluntary effort by people dedicated to the mission of the association. However again, voluntary effort by members and retired members of professional associations is somewhat different from that provided to distributing charities in that the identities of those providing the effort are marked by the reputation of the association by virtue of their individual professional status. The outcome of their efforts reflects on themselves in this intimate manner and in ways that they cannot completely control unless they resign and try to wipe away their past as a member of that profession. Volunteers within professional associations have this distinctive reason to 'care' about their association and about the outcome of their voluntary efforts.

3.4　Overall　regulatory　frameworks　for associations

Professional associations are constituted as not-for-profit organisations. However there are a number of special regulatory categories that associations can take on which give certain status, but require certain obligations and responsibilities. The most common in the UK were those with charitable status. Fewer had Royal Charters and very few were licensed in the sense that by law, individual practitioners had to belong to the association in order to practice. However there is some evidence that associations in the UK are moving towards both gaining charitable status and acquiring a Royal Charter. Table 3:4 provides this information for the UK and Ireland. The more general questions of whether associations were constituted as companies limited by guarantee and as statutory bodies were only asked in Ireland.

Table 3:4   Special forms of regulation

Special forms of regulation	% of respondents: UK	% of respondents: Ireland
Charitable status	47%	33%
Royal Charter	31%	5%
Licence to practice	5%	14%
Limited by guarantee	n/a	71%
Statutory body	n/a	5%

3.4.1   Charitable status

Charitable status in the UK allows tax benefits to organisations and to anyone who gives money to the organisation. The criteria for achieving charitable status as noted above are:

- First, that the purposes of the organisation must be exclusively and legally charitable. A charity cannot have some purposes that are charitable and others, which are not.

- Second, a charity must be for the benefit of the community or an appreciably important section of the community. It must have a public character. Benefit means that it must provide a net *'recognisable advantage for people at a level that reflects their needs'.* (See www.charity-commission.gov.uk/spr/corcom1.asp).

The Charity Commission is becoming more strict with its granting of charitable status. Currently organisations that relieve poverty, or advance education or religion are presumed to benefit the public. The new Charities Act of 2006[11] removes that presumption and therefore in future *'the public benefit of all charitable purposes would have to be demonstrated and not assumed'* (see www.charity-commission.gov.uk/spr/corcom1.asp).

---

[11] The Charities Act 2006 received royal assent in November 2006. The first group of provisions of the Act came into force on 27 February 2007.

Roughly half of the respondents in the UK, 47%, reported having charitable status. The proportion was lower in Ireland, but still substantial at 33%. The proportion of the 60 UK associations that responded positively to this question in both 2003 and in 2006, grew from 45% to 55%.[12] Among the 15 Irish associations that responded to both questionnaires the proportion that stated they had charitable status rose from 27% in 2003 to 40% in 2006. Thus charitable status seems to be on the rise among professional associations in both countries.

3.4.2   Royal Charter status

Royal Charters have existed for centuries. Traditionally they were given to cities or universities. Chartered status may be regarded as a badge of maturity of a professional body and a sign of having achieved a degree of professionalism. Royal Charters are administered through the Privy Council and are according to their website, *'granted very rarely these days'* (see www.privy-council.org.uk/output/Page45.asp).

It is stressed that each application is dealt with on its merits, however the Privy Council has published what it calls the 'main criteria' for granting a Royal Charter in the case of professional institutions (see www.privy-council.org.uk/output/Page45.asp). These are:

a) The institution should comprise members of a unique profession and should have most of those eligible as members, without significant overlap with other bodies.

b) Corporate members (meaning full individual members) should be qualified to at least first degree level in a relevant discipline.

c) The institution should be financially sound and able to demonstrate a track record of achievement over a number of years.

---

[12] In 2006 organisations were asked specifically whether they had a Royal Charter/ charitable status. In 2003 this information was elicited in conjunction with other questions (whether they were Unincorporated, Limited by shares, Limited by guarantee, Statutory body, other). However the comparison presented above is believed to be valid, that is, that there has been a move to achieve charitable status among UK professional associations in the past few years.

d) There needs to be a convincing case that it would be in the public interest to regulate the body in this way.

e) The institution is normally expected to be of substantial size (5000 members or more).

The Privy Council notes that the Charter is a form of government regulation and that it is costly for the government not only to grant Royal Charters, but also to maintain them in that future amendments to the Charter and by-laws of the professional association require Privy Council approval. One consequence of this is that, as a government regulated body, it must be shown that it is in the public interest to grant a Royal Charter. This underlies criterion d).

Another consequence of this is that it has to be, in a sense, worthwhile for the government to expend resources on regulating the professional association in this, rather costly, manner. It is therefore also important that the association be sustainable. We can interpret criteria a), c) and e) in terms of the sustainability of the professional association. Criteria e) and a) require the association to be substantial in terms of absolute size and size relative to the profession. These criteria, along with criterion c), require the institution to be both financially viable and significant.

A little under a third of associations in the UK, 31%, had a Royal Charter. As with charitable status slightly more, 35%, of those that responded to both 2006 and 2003 surveys had a Royal Charter in 2006 compared with only 30% of them that reported having a Royal Charter in 2003. Only one (5%) of respondents in Ireland had a Royal Charter. However, this is unusual as Ireland is a Republic.

Attitudes towards chartered status are changing in different ways. On one hand it seems that there is a growing opinion that a Royal Charter is a good thing for UK associations in particular. It gives kudos to the association and may be regarded as a draw for recruits to the profession, particularly from certain countries abroad (particularly Commonwealth countries). However, it may also be regarded as a drawback if chartered membership is expected for all or most of the members. It was noted in Friedman and Mason (2004a: 82-84), that in May 2002, the Institution of Electrical Engineers (IEE), now the Institution of Engineering and Technology (IET) decoupled chartered engineer status from membership of the institution; that is, in the past only those with chartered engineer status had voting rights in the institution.

> It was partly the feeling that in the twenty first century, having this kind of distinction was just out of step with the way people felt about things, you know the death of deference and so on, and partly a feeling that with the world moving ahead and a lot of our members moving into computing and areas where chartership was nothing like as important as it used to be ... that we should make ourselves relevant to people who were doing interesting worthwhile work but who didn't have to or didn't want to or couldn't become chartered.

(Friedman and Mason, 2004a: 83)

Another reason for this was in response to a change in employer attitudes; that some employers wanted to engage with one organisation to support the professional needs of all their technical staff.

3.4.3   License to practice

Only 5% of UK respondents reported that members had to belong to the association in order to practice. However the proportion in Ireland was higher, 14%. It is possible that this legal support for professional associations leads them to have a different attitude towards their members, perhaps less concerned with member material interests and more concerned with their professional status. The samples in this category were too small to test such a hypothesis.

- Chapter 4 -
Employment, management and operations

4.1   Introduction

The range of issues we could deal with here is vast. What follows concentrates on what we perceive to be the key issues. First we examine management of professional associations in the broad sense of managing through committees of primarily volunteers and then managing using paid staff, distinguishing full-time from part-time staff and distinguishing paid staff by location, that is, employment at head office compared with the regions and overseas. We also identify where the head office is located. Second, we examine the nature of the person who occupies the role of the top-level paid staff member: what title do they hold, what is their employment background and do they participate in the governing body?   Third, functions of professional associations are discussed, and fourth; we deal with the frequency of use of certain operational control tools. Following our overall theme of sustainability, we emphasise risk management and crisis management experiences of professional associations through a series of case studies in this chapter.

4.2   Management of association affairs by committee and using paid staff

The traditional model of the professional association is of a club-like organisation, governed by a Council of volunteers representing the membership and managed by them through committees answerable to the Council, composed primarily of volunteers. However, as associations grow, on one hand it becomes more and more difficult to organise the services members desire purely by volunteer effort, particularly those concerned with maintaining a register and developing IT and Internet requirements. On the other hand, sustainability of the organisation can be threatened by taking on fixed costs as represented by full-time paid staff and by setting up expectations within the membership of member service levels that can only be delivered by paid staff.

This sort of dilemma that small, but growing, professional associations face is explored in the next sections. PARN has been running a project on the 'growing pains' of smaller professional associations since early 2006. The first report on this ongoing project will be published later this year (see Williams with Woodhead, 2007).

4.2.1 Employment in relation to membership

Associations often rely on part-time staff. In the survey we distinguished full-time paid staff from full-time equivalent part-time staff. Table 4:1 shows the distribution of employment in the sample comparing full-time (FT) paid staff and part-time (PT) paid staff (measured as full-time equivalents [FTE]) according to bands of numbers of individual members for the UK. Table 4:2 shows the equivalent figures for Ireland. Clearly the number of staff is highly correlated with the number of individual members of the association. This correlation is particularly strong if we consider only organisations that are purely professional associations (see Tables 4:3 and 4:4).

Table 4:1   Employment in professional bodies by size of membership of individuals: UK

Size of organisation by number of individual members	Mean number of FT paid staff	Mean number of FTE PT paid staff	Mean total staff	Number of respondents
Less than 1500	7.9	1.6	9.5	18
1501 to 3000	2.4	2.4	4.7	11
3001 to 5000	9.9	5.1	15.1	17
5001-20000	36.8	5.6	42.4	24
More than 20000	149.4	14.7	164.1	19
Total	45.6	6.2	51.8	89

Table 4:2   Employment in professional bodies by size of membership of individuals: Ireland

Size of organisation by number of individual members	Mean number of FT paid staff	Mean number of FTE PT paid staff	Mean total staff	Number of respondents
Less than 1500	2.0	2.0	4.0	8
1501 to 3000	7.8	1.3	9.0	4
3001 to 5000	-	-	-	0
5001-20000	10.5	0.5	11.0	2
More than 20000	-	-	-	0
Total	4.9	1.6	6.4	14

There is a clear relationship between size by individual members and number of full-time staff. The relationship is less clear, but still there for part-time staff. One complication is that the proportion of staff to individual members is distorted at the smaller end (i.e. less than 1500 members in the UK sample) because of associations (which are both professional associations and trade associations in particular) with a large proportion of company members. In order to remove this factor Tables 4:3 and 4:4 show the figures for the UK and Ireland, but only for respondents that identified themselves as only professional associations, that is, as 'pure' professional associations. In these tables the relation is clearly consistent and strong throughout the membership distribution. Another point that is clear is how the ratio of full-time to part-time staff rises with the size of the association. For the very small associations the proportion of staff working full-time is less or roughly the same as the proportion of staff that are part-time, as measured by full-time equivalents. Above 1500 members in Ireland and above 3000 members in the UK and the proportion of full-time staff outnumbers part-time staff substantially, by roughly between 5:1 and 20:1.

Table 4:3   Employment in 'pure' professional associations by size of membership of individuals: UK

Size of organisation by number of individual members	Mean number of FT paid staff	Mean number of FTE PT paid staff	Mean total staff	Number of respondents
Less than 1500	1.0	1.2	2.2	9
1501 to 3000	2.1	2.1	4.2	9
3001 to 5000	11.5	1.3	12.8	12
5001-20000	25.4	5.8	31.2	13
More than 20000	217.7	25.0	242.7	3
Total	25.0	4.3	29.2	46

Table 4:4   Employment in 'pure' professional associations by size of membership of individuals: Ireland

Size of organisation by number of individual members	Mean number of FT paid staff	Mean number of FTE PT paid staff	Mean total staff	Number of respondents
Less than 1500	1.0	0.5	1.5	4
1501 to 3000	7.8	1.3	9.0	4
3001 to 5000	-	-	-	0
5001-20000	10.5	0.5	11.0	2
More than 20000	-	-	-	0
Total	5.6	0.8	6.4	10

4.2.2 Management by committee

Many professional associations are still managed on volunteer effort through committees attached to and led by members of the governing body. Tables 4:3 and 4:4 show that professional associations with less than 1,500 members in the UK and Ireland, get along with on average only one full-time staff member. In fact 6% of respondents to the 2006 PARN survey in the UK had no staff at all, 5% employed only part-time staff (base of 98 answered these questions). Comparable figures for the Irish survey were 12.5% with no staff at all and 6.3% with only part-time staff out of a base of 16 who answered these questions. These estimates of 11% of UK and 19% of Irish associations which are run entirely on voluntary effort, or with only minimal part-time paid support is certainly an underestimate of the proportions so run in the population of professional associations in these countries. We presume that such associations would find it more difficult to resource filling out the questionnaire. Also, as noted in Chapter 1, the PARN database is least complete for associations of this size, which are difficult to identify because of their smaller or absent footprint on the Internet or in directories, and they are less likely to have the resources to identify themselves to PARN.

It is worth pointing out that even those associations with say three or less full-time (or full-time equivalent part-timers) are likely to be largely run by committees, primarily or entirely composed of volunteers.

Will those who volunteer to carry out activities required for the execution of the aims and objects of the association in fact deliver what they have promised? Many will also have paid jobs. Also what some promise to do for the association may require skills and experience that they do not have. In addition, the means of disciplining volunteers is limited, at least financially. If they do not deliver what is promised, in the time and in the manner required, what can the governing body or paid managers do?

Management of volunteer effort, if it is primarily carried out through committees of the governing body, can be problematic. Management by committee will be more intermittent than by paid full-time managers. Decision making is traditionally slower and less flexible through committees. Also over time the likelihood of overlapping responsibilities among different committees grows over time as more activities are taken on. Committees can proliferate if they are set up for particular purposes and then become permanent because disbanding a committee of volunteers can be difficult. However, on the other hand volunteers are likely to be enthusiastic and many will be more able than staff associations could afford to hire. There is also likely to be a greater sense of solidarity with the association among the membership if a substantial proportion of members are involved in its management and operations.

Tables 4:5 and 4:6 show the distribution of committees for both samples in the UK and Ireland. On average associations in the UK had 8.4 permanent committees with the median number of 5. In Ireland on average associations had 7.3 permanent committees with a median of 5.

Table 4:5 Number of permanent committees: UK

	Number of respondents	Number of permanent committees				
		0	**1-3**	**4-6**	**7-9**	**10+**
% of respondents	99	1%	30%	39%	12%	17%
Average number of members	99	75	7209	9762	60624	37830
Permanent Committees as a % of membership	99	0	0.13%	0.13%	0.08%	0.29%
Committee as % membership for smaller associations (<3000 members)	32	0	0.31%	0.42%	0.33%	1.67%

Table 4:6 Number of permanent committees: Ireland

	Number of respondents	Number of permanent committees				
		0	1-3	4-6	7-9	10+
% of respondents	19	0	37%	26%	16%	21%
Average number of members	19	-	2811	2542	1300	2256
Permanent Committees as a % of membership	19	-	0.14%	0.4%	2%	1%
Committee as % membership for smaller associations (<3000 members)	14	-	0.2%	0.5%	2%	2%

Smaller associations, those with less than 3000 members, have a higher ratio of permanent committees to members. This is particularly so for the sample of UK associations where the ratio of the ratios ranged from over 2:1 for those with only 1-3 committees (comparing .31% to .13%) to almost 6:1 for those with more than 10 committees (comparing .29% to 1.67%). Irish associations in the overall sample have considerably more permanent committees, however, looking only at associations with less than 3000 members in both countries shows only a somewhat higher ratio of permanent committees to members, primarily due to a few Irish associations with very large numbers of permanent committees.

Overall, 36% of the UK sample reported having a formal procedure for evaluating the purpose, effectiveness and value of permanent committees. A similar proportion, 40% stated that they had a formal procedure for disbanding permanent committees. However, only 69% of those, that is, 26% of the total sample, confirmed that they had ever used this procedure to disband a permanent committee. The equivalent figures for Ireland were 29% having a formal procedure for evaluating permanent committees, 52% had a formal procedure for disbanding permanent committees, but only 60% of those, or 30% of the total sample, had ever used the procedure to disband a permanent committee.

4.2.3 Management through employed staff

The number of full-time paid staff of associations varied from 0 to 540 employees among UK respondents and from 0 to 140 for Irish respondents. Employment of staff is a major issue for smaller professional associations. On one hand having paid staff reduces the vulnerability of the professional association to potential vicissitudes of voluntary effort noted above. On the other hand employed staff must also be regarded as an overhead and ultimately a danger to the sustainability of a professional body if things go badly. Clearly management issues differ depending on whether most of the operations of an association are carried out by volunteers or paid staff.

The following case study demonstrates some of the issues involved in making the transition from management by committee to management by employed staff.

4.2.4 Case study on the transition from a voluntarily run to a professionally staffed organisation: The Society of Indexers

Case Study 4:1
Based on an interview with Ann Kingdom - Marketing Director (formerly Honorary Secretary), The Society of Indexers, February 2007.

The Society of Indexers is a relatively small organisation with around 800 members. In 2007 they had two administrators working for them, one full time and one working 30 hours a week, as well as at least 30 volunteers undertaking specific tasks (and others serving on committees). This is an increase since 2004, when they only had ¾ of a person being paid to work for them and most tasks were undertaken by volunteers. They have had part-time administrative staff since the mid-1990s, when they were sharing an office and Administrator with another organisation in London. They moved their office to Sheffield in 1999, took on a new part-time Administrator and moved some tasks formerly done by volunteers into the office. At this time they discussed the advantages of employing a Chief Executive but this was not a serious option due to financial considerations. However, it became clear that it would be necessary to increase the hours of their existing member of staff. They employed an assistant on a casual basis and gradually upped the administrator's hours until she became full-time in 2006 and her assistant was given a permanent contract. The Administrator was at that time the most senior member of paid staff and had no professional background in indexing.

The catalyst for this change came during 2003 and 2004 when they commissioned an in-depth review of the whole organisation. It was done by a relatively new member with an accountancy background. He had the advantage of being able to look at the organisation in a fairly independent manner but was able to provide his services at favourable rates. The review highlighted some potential problems within the organisation such as overlapping committee membership and inefficient communication between the volunteers and between volunteers and paid staff. It also established that there was a need for more centralisation to reduce the burden on the overworked volunteers and provide a more efficient and consistent service. To this end, it recommended that they should completely reorganise the committee structure and be looking to employ two full-time members of paid staff; this is what they worked towards over the next few years.

One advantage to having the two members of staff is a significant reduction of pressure on the volunteers, particularly for the Secretary and Treasurer (the latter had previously had to spend a lot of his time on basic book-keeping). The administrative staff have now become much more directly involved with the organisation and all its activities, which has been extremely beneficial. They are able to answer more queries themselves rather than passing them onto somebody else and the expansion in hours has meant that they have time to actually attend some committee meetings, so they can have more input at the policy-making level, which is very useful and makes the job much more rewarding. Not only this, but there is the added advantage of having two people working together who can bounce ideas off one another and provide each other with support. As Ann Kingdom, the former Secretary of the Society, commented: "A happy administrator is a happy Society."

Another big advantage is that members are now getting a better service. During the transition, the Society tried to consult with its members and keep them in the picture so that they understood what they were doing and why.

The only problems Ann mentioned about increasing paid staff is that people now tend to assume that the office can do everything and may pass on work to the staff without checking whether they have the capacity to do it in the time required: "Nobody really realises just how much goes on in the office, because most of the volunteers haven't actually been to the office and seen it working."

In theory the Honorary Secretary is the 'line manager' responsible for the office; however, as freelance indexers the Society's officers generally do not have this type of managerial experience. Ann mentioned that it would be beneficial to have an experienced employee at a higher level for this type of role.

Inevitably they have had to increase member subscription fees, but this has not had a huge effect on membership numbers. The review considered how much they could feasibly increase subscriptions in order to pay for more staff time. It did require a big jump in fees in one year, but now they have a small annual increase.

The Society still relies heavily on the goodwill of many volunteers but they are generally glad not to have to do some of the administrative work they were burdened with previously. There is still the problem that volunteers sometimes do not deliver, but Ann believes "It's not a lack of motivation, but just a lack of time", because they have to balance their paid indexing work with doing (unpaid) work for the Society. To deal with this problem, and ensure that jobs are done professionally, some volunteers are paid realistic fees, particularly for training-related activities such as marking test papers or running workshops; others such as the journal and newsletter editors receive honoraria. The Society previously had an elaborate system of honoraria but this was abandoned as it was increasingly seen as unfair:

> Paying an honorarium for being a committee chair makes no difference to whether somebody's going to do it or not. In relation to the time they spend, it's nothing, but when you add them all up it's quite an outlay for the Society, so it seemed best to scrap most of them.

The Society of Indexers recognise that in order that the relationships between volunteers and paid staff function properly it is necessary to establish formal roles and responsibilities for everyone. They now have detailed job descriptions for every position and these are reviewed regularly.

As well as increasing staff hours, they have also increased the amount of outsourcing they do, rather than hoping to find volunteers with the right skills within the membership. They now outsource the typesetting of their newsletter to a professional typesetter, for example, and Ann believes that further expansion in this area might be the way to go in the future.

Overall, by having more paid staff the public face of the society is now that of a professionally run society. However, despite the advantages the administrators have brought, the Society still lacks someone to take on an executive role. Volunteers still have to take on much of what a Chief Executive would normally do and they do not always have the necessary expertise for tasks such as developing a proper business plan. Along with making the deputy Administrator full-time, appointing a Chief Executive may be the next step, but it is unlikely that the problems of cost can be overcome in the near future.

Ann believes that in managing a transition like this, communication is vital, not only between paid staff and volunteer staff, but also with the members: *"Problems are almost always to do with a breakdown in communication. It can lead to resentment and really undermine what you are trying to do."*

4.2.5 Overall employment by location

According to the 2006 sample in the UK, most professional associations (54%) have their primary head office (HO) in London. In addition, 12% had their head office in the South East, but outside London. The only other substantial area with head offices was the Midlands, with 16%. Notably there were only 4% in Scotland and none in Wales or Northern Ireland. However 28% of the sample had some head office functions outside their primary HO location. Of these 7% mentioned offices in all three other devolved countries, 3% mentioned offices in Scotland and Wales only and a further 27% only mentioned Scotland.

A number of professional associations have mentioned to PARN that they have noticed an upsurge of interest in Scotland from their own offices, particularly with respect to being close to the relatively new Scottish parliament. However this was not reflected in a change from 2003 survey. In fact, examining only responses of the 61 that answered this question in both surveys, the proportion with head offices in Wales,

Scotland and Northern Ireland remained exactly the same. In fact the only changes to the answers was a shift of two associations from head offices in East Anglia, one to the Midlands and one to the South East outside of London. The other trend that was noted in our analysis of location for the 2003 survey (Friedman and Mason, 2004a: 57), the decentralisation of head offices from London to the regions does not register in the comparisons of head office locations between the 2003 and 2006 surveys. Of the 61 exactly the same proportion of head offices (just over half, 55%) were in London. This may reflect a rise in congestion and cost of office space outside of London in the main areas that professional associations would like to relocate to. It may reflect a move that was not picked up by our question, which would be moves from central London to London suburbs (though one of our options was South East outside of London).

The Irish associations were overwhelmingly based in Dublin, 17 of the 21 respondents or 81%.

We also distinguished employment by location of staff, that is, whether staff were primarily located at head office, in the regions/branches or overseas. The mean and quartile figures for those employed at these locations are shown in Table 4:7 for the UK and Table 4:8 for Ireland.

Table 4:7 Employment in associations by location and if full-time: UK

Location and if full-time in UK		Number of employees or FTEs			Sample size
		Mean	1st quartile	3rd quartile	
Full-time	At head office	38.9	3	42	106
	In regions/ branches	16.2	0	5.5	69
	Overseas	4.7	0	0	61
Part-time FTEs	At head office	10.7	1	4	99
	In regions/ branches	4.3	0	2.8	64
	Overseas	1.7	0	0	55

Table 4:8 Employment in associations by location and if full-time: Ireland

Location and if full-time in Ireland		Number of employees or FTEs			Sample size
		Mean	1st quartile	3rd quartile	
Full-time	At head office	13	1	9	19
	In regions/ branches	0.1	0	0	10
	Overseas	0	0	0	10
Part-time FTEs	At head office	3.4	0	2.3	18
	In regions/ branches	1.1	0	0	9
	Overseas	0	0	0	9

On average most staff are employed full-time and at head office. This is overwhelmingly so in Ireland. In the UK, on average this only accounted for half of the full-time and full-time equivalent part-time employees. Overall 65% of staff resource of UK associations is located at head office, 26% in regions/branches and 9% overseas. However as can be seen from the quartile information very few UK associations had any staff overseas (and none of the Irish associations had overseas staff). Only 18% reported having any full-time staff overseas and only 13% had any part-time staff. Only 43% reported having any full-time staff in regions/branches and only 42% had any part-time staff there. While 89% reported having some full-time staff at head office and 81% had part-time staff at head office.

Table 4:9 shows the distribution of employment for part-time staff as a percentage of all staff by location and for different sizes of associations by membership for the UK. Overall the proportion of part-time staff (as measured by full-time equivalents) to total paid staff was 25.4% in the UK. This is based on 83 respondents.

Table 4:9   Ratios of part-time to total staff by size of association for professional associations: UK

% FTE PT paid staff by location	Size of organisation					Total
	Less than 1500 individual members	1500-3000 individual members	3001-5000 individual members	5001-20000 individual members	More than 20000 individual members	
Head office	41.3%	59.4%	22.4%	11.5%	7.6%	23.1%
Region	60%	88.9%	85.7%	38.1%	25.2%	43.5%
Overseas	0%	-	100%	100%	18%	32.6%
Overall	44.5%	59.3%	24.8%	14.9%	9.2%	25.4%

The proportion of part-timers is higher in the regions than at head office among UK associations for all size bands. The difference is particularly marked for associations, which are in the middle size ranges, that is those with between 1500 and 20000 members. Associations which employ people overseas overwhelmingly use part-timers for those with 20000 members or less, but once the association reaches a size whereby it may be considered an international organisation, the proportion of part-timers falls to a similar level overseas as it is in the regions of the UK.

4.3   Case study on outsourcing: The Institute of Management Consultants and Advisors

One alternative to employing staff is to use volunteers. Another is to outsource certain functions of the association. This can allow small associations to provide services with limited management resources. Case study 4:2 depicts a small association that has successfully gone down this path.

Case study 4:2
Based on an interview with Eoin O'Shea – former President, The
Institute of Management Consultants and Advisors, February 2007.

The Institute of Management Consultants and Advisors (IMCA) is a small Irish organisation with about 600 members. Up until 2006 they had no Chief Executive or administration staff. In 2006 they took on a part-time Membership Development Executive who works roughly half a day a week to try to recruit new members. They now have 20 volunteers working for them. In order to cope with the lack of paid staff of their own, they commission Price Waterhouse Coopers (PWC) on an annual charge to work for them. The outsourcing arrangement is something that the organisation has always done, but they changed to PWC from a previous arrangement which was *"an affiliate type arrangement with a business body"*. They outsource mainly small administrative tasks to PWC such as answering the phone, emails and letters, as well as monitoring the membership database and finance. The reason they do not employ anyone themselves to do this is mainly due to financial costs, however Eoin O'Shea, the President of the Institute until late 2006, said that even if they did employ somebody themselves they would still outsource to cover when their people are away or on sick leave.

In order to decide which company to use for outsourcing they consulted their members who came back with three or four proposals and PWC was chosen for its professional reputation. Up until now they have found the arrangement very satisfactory and can see few drawbacks other than the fact that the Council are responsible for everything. Eoin believes that they will continue with this arrangement in the future, even if they take on a chief executive: *"Whatever you do would be in addition to the backup administrative arrangement."*

4.4   Top management

As professional associations move from being run by volunteers to using paid full-time staff, changes will occur in the nature of the top person hired. One aspect of the change will be the role of the top manager. We have tried to capture this by asking about the title of the most senior salaried member of staff. Our presumption is that as associations develop they will move from hiring someone to manage operations to someone who will take on a more strategic role. We regard this as supporting the professionalisation of professional associations. Another aspect of change is the background and experience of the top salaried position. This we tried to capture by asking what was their previous employment.

4.4.1   Title of most senior salaried member of staff

Table 4:10 shows the distribution of job titles for the most senior member of staff. There were 103 in the UK and 19 in Ireland that answered this question.

Chief Executive is the clear preference among job titles for the most senior salaried member of staff. This was more common than all other titles together, both in the UK and in Ireland. Positions indicating clearly lower level positions; Office Manager, Administrative Secretary and Chief Operating Officer accounted together for 10% of titles among UK respondents, but for 21% among Irish respondents, reflecting the smaller size of the sample of Irish respondents. Many of the other titles represent more a difference in customary terminology than a difference in level.

Table 4:10 Job titles for most senior salaried staff position

Job title	% of sample: UK	% of those with title who have been a qualified professional member of the association: UK	% of sample: Ireland	% of those with title who have been a qualified professional member of the association: Ireland
Chief Executive	60%	44%	58%	30%
Director General	9%	44%	11%	100%
Secretary General	9%	56%	5%	0
Executive Officer	4%	50%	5%	100%
Administrative Secretary	4%	25%	5%	0
Chief Operating Officer	3%	33%	5%	100%
Office Manager	3%	33%	11%	0
Other most senior salaried staff position	9%	78%	0	0

It is interesting that what we would regard to be a common pattern of stages in the development of the top salaried position role at professional associations, does not hold in all cases. We have had in mind the idea that a professional body typically follows the following stages:

1.   Beginning as entirely volunteer run;

2.   Take on part-time and temporary staff for primarily administrative roles, which are managed by volunteers.

3. Hire the first full-time staff member in the role of office manager to coordinate the efforts of the operational support staff and then to fill in hiring more operational staff.

4. Hire someone to take a more executive role, both in leading the full-time staff more actively and to liaise with the governing body on strategic matters. At this point the top salaried staff member would attend governing body meetings, but not have voting rights.

5. Eventually they would acquire voting rights, though this would probably be accompanied by a change in the structure of the governing body from a single Council to a smaller Board.

6. Some have taken this process a further step and come to be run by a small Executive Committee, which contains a mix of paid staff and volunteers. In this governance the association comes to resemble the governance of private companies.

However we note that these stages are not always followed and we do not regard it as inevitable that associations will always follow this pattern to the end, or even to near the end. There are arguments for stopping at each of these stages, though we generally believe that 'progress' would be achieved by moving from step 1 through to step 4 as the association membership grows.

Moving through stages 4, 5 and 6 raises a critical issue. Who speaks for the association? Is it the top paid staff member, the Chief Executive or Executive Director, or is it the top volunteer, the Chair of Council or President. One association reported on in Friedman and Mason (2004a: 55) moved quickly from step 2 to step 4 and then decided to 'move back' to step 3 (or 2). When the Executive Director left, a part-time Office Manager replaced him.

4.4.2   Background of most senior salaried member of staff

We also asked if the person in the top staff position had been a qualified professional member of the association. Interestingly while roughly half of the higher level job titles for the UK sample, were occupied by people who had been a qualified professional member of the association in question, only a quarter or a third of the lower level titles were occupied by a qualified professional member. There are possibly two different factors here. On one hand, some of the lower level top jobs are taken up by administrators, by people who are at a support level and would be considered at a lower level than professional members. However, a new trend may be that for the top jobs for chief executives are moving towards a situation where associations consider the person who runs their association as needing to be qualified for that job, as opposed to qualified in what the members of the association do. This may be considered to be an indicator of a more professional attitude towards the management of the professional association (though clearly not in all cases, particularly when the profession itself is in the business and management area).

The other category was surprisingly out of line with the rest of the sample with a very high proportion who were qualified professional members of the association. This is in part due to several of the 'other' positions specified were volunteer positions, president, head of professional development. Others that answered in this category noted that they only had part-time staff.

In a separate question respondents were asked about the previous employment of the person occupying the top salaried position in the association. Table 4:11 shows the options that were offered to respondents for the UK. That table compares the background of the top salaried position for all the different job titles. The most common previous position for Chief Executives was as a 'practising professional in the sector', accounting for a third of the sample in the UK and 37% of the Irish sample. Only 9% of the UK sample came from a different paid role at their own organisation, and none in the Irish sample. A quarter came from a similar role at another type of organisation and 19% came from a similar role at another professional association. For the Irish sample 32% came from a similar role in another type of organisation, while only 5% came from a similar role in another professional association.

We suspect that these latter two categories, which accounted for just under half of the UK sample will become more important in future. In particular the proportion taking on the top job at a professional association from a similar role at another professional association may be taken as an indication of the professional association sector coming to recognise itself as such. That is, that running or participating in running one association is good experience for running another one.

Table 4:11   Past jobs by job title: UK

Job title	% of sample	Similar role at another professional association	Similar role at another type of organisation	Different paid role at your organisation	Practicing professional in your sector	Other
Chief Executive	60%	16%	28%	8%	33%	18%
Director General	9%	22%	22%	0	22%	33%
Secretary General	9%	44%	11%	22%	33%	0
Executive Officer	4%	0	0	50%	25%	25%
Administrative Secretary	4%	0	50%	0	50%	25%[*]
Chief Operating Officer	3%	0	0	0	33%	67%
Office Manager	3%	33%	33%	0	33%	33%
Other	9%	25%	25%	0	50%	13%
Total	**100%**	**19%**	**25%**	**9%**	**34%**	**20%**
Sample size	*103*	*19*	*25*	*9*	*34*	*20*

[*] Note that rows may add up to more than 100% due to respondents ticking more than one option.

Tables 4:12 and 4:13 also compare the background of the most senior salaried staff, but only for two groups of job titles: those imply a strategic role compared with those that imply a more administrative or operational role. This makes it clear that for the UK and especially for Ireland, the proportion of top staff individuals with lower level titles coming from the 'Other' category is much higher than for top staff individuals with higher level titles. As noted above, the 'other' positions were often volunteer positions at the association. These were situations when a volunteer was persuaded to take on the office functions of the association as a paid employee, full-time or part-time.

Table 4:12 Comparison of previous employment of most senior staff in UK: strategic role vs. administrative or operational role

Job title	% of sample	Similar role at another professional association	Similar role at another type of organisation	Different paid role at your organisation	Practicing professional in your sector	Other
Chief Executive/ Director General/ Secretary General/ Executive Officer	87%	19%	24%	10%	33%	17%
Administrative Secretary/ Chief Operating Officer/ Office Manager	14%	15%	31%	0	39%	39%

Table 4:13 Comparison of previous employment of most senior staff in Ireland: strategic role vs. administrative or operational role

Job title	% of sample	Similar role at another professional association	Similar role at another type of organisation	Different paid role at your organisation	Practicing professional in your sector	Other
Chief Executive/ Director General/ Secretary General/ Executive Officer	79%	7%	40%	0	47%	7%
Administrative Secretary/ Chief Operating Officer/ Office Manager	21%	0	0	0	0	100%

4.5   Operational control procedures

4.5.1   Financial management tools

Respondents were asked if any of the following financial management tools or procedures were in place in their organisation. In the UK the results were that almost all, 91%, had business plans, 58% had risk management systems and 53% carried out internal audits. For Ireland the proportions were 55% had business plans, 15% had risk management systems and 40% carried out internal audits. Thus a substantially lower proportion of Irish associations had business plans and risk management systems, though the difference in proportions with internal audits was much closer between Ireland and the UK. Members in Ireland suggested that formal external audit be added to the list of possible financial management tools when the survey came to be distributed in Ireland. Of the 20 who answered the question 85% indicated that they did use this method. We did not ask this question in the UK, however we suspect that a high proportion in the UK would also have formal external audit.

In Chapter 8 we compare use of these financial management tools by size of association between UK and Irish associations. We find that though some of the difference between their usage of these tools can be attributed to the smaller size of Irish associations, there is still a difference in general in usage of these tools when UK and Irish associations of the same size are compared (as measured by number of full-time equivalent paid staff).

Using the incidence of these financial management tools as one indicator of the progress of the professionalisation of professional associations, it would appear that UK associations have progressed further as a sector than those in Ireland.

For the 50 that answered these questions in both 2003 and 2006 surveys in the UK, there was a marked increase in internal audit, from 50% to 60% and an increase in risk management, from 70% to 76% from 2003 to 2006. Those saying they had business plans declined slightly from 94% to 92%. The overall percentages are net figures that conceal much more substantial changes among the associations between the two surveys. While there was a net decrease of one association carrying out business plans, 5 associations made changes, either to introduce business plans or to abandon them. While there was a net increase of three associations which had introduced risk management systems, 12 associations actually made changes. The net increase in numbers taking on internal audit was five but almost half the respondents, 21, either introduced them or abandoned them. Tables 4:14 and 4:15 show the changes for the 25 in the UK that had changed their use of financial management tools and the 8 in Ireland that did. There was much less change among the Irish respondents, even taking account of the lower sample size.

Table 4:14 Changes in use of financial management tools, 2003 and 2006: UK

Financial management tools	2003 proportion	2006 proportion	Changes
Business plan	94%	92%	
No business plan to business plan			+2
Business plan to no business plan			-3
Risk management	70%	76%	
No risk manage to risk manage			+8
Risk manage to no risk manage			-4
Internal audit	50%	60%	
No internal audit to internal audit			+13
Internal audit to no internal audit			-8

Table 4:15 Changes in use of financial management tools, 2003 and 2006: Ireland

Financial management tools	2003 proportion	2006 proportion	Changes
Business Plan	75%	75%	
No business plan to business plan			+1
Business plan to no business plan			-1
Risk Management	25%	38%	
No risk manage to risk manage			+1
Risk manage to no risk manage			-0
Internal Audit	75%	63%	
No internal audit to internal audit			+0
Internal audit to no internal audit			-1

4.5.2 Case study on risk management: The Institution of Occupational Safety and Health

As noted in Chapter 2, we regard risk management as an important component in developing strategies for sustainability of professional associations. Case 4:3 provides some insight into a successful risk management system at an association where one would expect a sophisticated system to be in place.

Case study 4:3
Based on an interview with Colin Gore - Director of Finance and Corporate Services, Institution of Occupational Safety and Health.

The Institution of Occupational Safety and Health (IOSH) is a large organisation with over 30000 members. Their risk management plan was set up between 2001 and 2002 as a result of the introduction of SORP 2000 which came out in October 2000. This is the Statement of Recommended Practice, a requirement of charity reporting which obliges trustees of all charities to make a statement that: *"the major risks to which the charity is exposed, as identified by the trustees, have been reviewed and systems have been established to mitigate those risks."*

Before this the only arrangements they had were informal and not recorded. But they do recognise that it is good management to have a risk management plan in place. At a meeting in 2001 the Institute's Auditor gave a presentation to Committee members about SORP 2000 and the risk management process. Following this Colin Gore gave a similar presentation to all employees. All members of staff took part in a brainstorming session of what risks they faced and then the senior management team worked on these, giving them a weighting of how likely they were to take place. This stage in formulating the plan was done entirely internally. Things which can control risk such as taking out insurance were seen as management decisions as Colin Gore commented: *"I didn't feel we needed external consultants, because we know, or we should know our risks better than external people because we know our business better."*

But IOSH also have the advantage that many of the committee members are in fact risk managers because they are health and safety practitioners, so a lot can be done through the Committee.

At that time the main risks identified were IT/loss of data, terrorism, fire, loss of key customers and adverse publicity. Since the change in governance structure which saw the introduction of a risk management and audit committee other risks have emerged, for example the loss of senior management team members. This was something suggested by the committee which senior management themselves had not considered. The risk management and audit committee meets four times a year. Before its formation the risk management process would be reported through to the audit committee as it then was, who would report once a year to the Council. Now the risk management and audit committee report to the board of trustees who then make a statement in the annual account.

IOSH's risk management plan is very much a live document. It is formally reviewed by the risk management and audit committee once a year, but the senior management committee tend to look at it twice a year. It is modified every time it is reviewed to incorporate any new risks that have been identified. At the time they were embarking on a major information systems project, and a new risk of the possibility of the software not working after a large amount of money has been spent, has been identified. The only means of testing the risk management plan that was in place at that time was regular review. Table top exercises for this aspect of risk management are something IOSH would be interested in introducing if time constraints allowed.

IOSH measure risk by looking both at measures of control available to avoid the threat occurring, and areas of mitigation that would lessen the effect if it were to occur. The risk management plan has come under scrutiny on two occasions recently, one being after the loss of a major customer. Control and mitigating factors are scored on a four point scale for each risk and they found, in this particular case, that they had underestimated the risk prior to control and mitigating factors. The second occasion was when the computer systems went down. In this case the plan successfully held up.

IOSH have been working on a new emergency plan for a couple of years, and this was put to the risk management and audit committee in 2005. It includes setting up an emergency team, comprising the Director of Communications, the Director of Finance and Corporate Services, the Facilities Manager, the IT manager and the HR manager, the Chief Executive is often involved as well. In 2006 a trustee who was a risk manager was invited to conduct a table top exercise. He thought of two or three different scenarios and they decided as a team what actions they would take. Afterwards they worked on a number of issues which arose from this and reported back to the risk management and audit committee. They have also placed key information and contacts such as banks and insurers in an offsite location.

The name for the emergency plan was debated internally and around the committee. Many people have called it disaster recovery, but crisis management was not considered. As Colin Gore said: *"I think 'crisis' is rather a negative word compared to emergency, but it depends on your point of view"*. Whatever name it is given, IOSH see it as being a critical subset of risk management.

The only difficulty in development of this plan is in how it can be tested, since closing the business in order to have practice runs of possible events is too costly: *"It is being developed academically, in that you are trying to think about your obvious scenarios and it's not until you have a real example that you can actually test it."*

The success of the risk management plan for IOSH was in part down to an excellent committee who have identified some very testing questions. Furthermore Colin Gore sees buy-in from senior management, a regular review and viewing the plan as a real piece of work as critical for success: *"There's always a danger that not everybody can get enthusiastic about risk management. But all of the senior management team have a role to play."*

4.5.3   Crisis management

Crisis management is the process of working through a crisis, or solving problems as they arise, though such situations should also be considered in a risk management system. Crisis management has become an important issue, particularly in the light of the July 2005 London bombings. We would regard a crisis management plan to be part of the armoury of any organisation taking a professional approach to its management and obviously for an organisation concerned with its sustainability. In May 2006 PARN issued a member enquiry asking the following questions:

- Do you have a formal crisis management plan, which has been passed on to staff members?

- How did you formulate this plan – do you have internal staff or use consultants?

- What would you recommend from the process you have followed and what might you change?

We received 17 responses from 15 associations in the UK and 2 in Ireland. Of these, 7 respondents stated that they had a formal crisis management plan, but sometimes this was part of a larger plan encompassing crisis management. These were named:

- business continuity plan

- business recovery plan

- disaster recovery plan

- risk strategy plan

The contents of these plans varied. Here are some examples of features of particular association strategies:

- Key parts of the plan deal with communication surrounding the handling of the crisis so all stakeholders are kept informed at regular intervals of how the association is coping with the crisis.

- Plan includes off-site business recovery facilities, instructions to staff on how to access these facilities and a team of managers who would deal with the effects of any incident.

- Plan is supported by financial policy that establishes reserves to enable the organisation to continue to meet its financial obligations for a three-month period even if all sources of income stop suddenly.

- Plan contains a series of scenarios to provide guidance on dealing with a range of incidents.

- An in-house business continuity team meets regularly to continuously develop the plan and to monitor the environment within which the association operates for potential crisis e.g. pandemics.

A small number (4) used external consultants to support internal staff in developing the crisis management plan. One also mentioned using the

City of London Contingency Planning division and 'London Prepared' - a government backed information website (see http://www.londonprepared.gov.uk).

Recommendations included:

- Early involvement of the correct staff, including senior management.

- A full recovery rehearsal.

- Embedding crisis management in core planning and performance management systems; monitor the risk register quarterly, as part of the regular operational planning cycle.

- Keep the design documents of the plans up to date and relevant, brief, succinct and to the point, *'cut out irrelevant information'*.

4.5.4   Case study on crisis management: The Institute of Highways and Transportation

This case study is particularly interesting as it comes from an association that found itself in the real crisis of the July 2005 London bombings.

Case study 4:4
Based on an interview with Mary Lewis - Chief Executive, The Institute of Highways and Transportation, February 2007

The head office of the Institute of Highways and Transportation (IHT) is located around the corner from Tavistock Square in Central London, the location of the bus bomb on 7th July 2005. It is a fairly small office with around 20 members of staff, but was badly affected on the day of the bomb and for about two weeks afterwards, because initially they could not gain access to the building, and thereafter were within the 'exclusion zone'. This meant they could not receive deliveries (including post), and all staff had to identify themselves against lists held by the police as they came to work each morning, all of which significantly restricted their activities.

They have had a basic crisis management plan in place since around 2003, formulated entirely by the Chief Executive of the IHT Mary Lewis, without going through the trustees. Before being appointed to this role she had worked for the Chartered Institute of Bankers, which was based in the late 80s and 90s in the City of London. During this time, she often met with the Metropolitan Police who took crisis management very seriously. Bringing this experience to her new role, Mary's crisis management plan was met mainly with apathy from other members of staff.

The initial plan was severely tested on the day of the bomb. It had made certain assumptions about what a crisis might be and little applied to real life. The basic principles, such as the place where everyone would gather in case of a bomb, did however hold up. It had assumed that personnel would not be able to gain access to the building and was geared towards keeping the business running if this was the case. In fact the exact opposite to this happened. Most of the staff were in the building at the time and the problem they faced was not being able to leave and not having communication with the outside world. Those who had not arrived at work at the time of the bomb could not reach the office, and could not communicate to tell the office that they were safe. Mary Lewis emphasised that it was the small details that are generally overlooked when designing the plan. For example how to contact people when mobile phone networks are down, and keeping emergency supplies of food in the building: *"The true lesson was how easy it is to make assumptions about what can comprise a crisis."*

After the event the audit committee and other members of staff took the need for a crisis management plan much more seriously. The new plan is more flexible and the changes made include making sure that everybody has everybody else's contact number, equipment in the office has been rethought, introducing a radio to find out what is going on, and a 24-hour emergency supply of food. They now have the ability to control the service from outside the office and have reconfigured the telephone system, so that they can continue receiving landline calls direct in the 'safe area' in a crisis. They also have an informal arrangement with the organisation that publish their magazine, based in Tunbridge Wells, who now keep a record of crucial documents such as insurance details in their office, avoiding the need for anyone having to take responsibility for these things in the IHT office in case of a crisis. This would only apply to smaller organisations that have one office.

The crisis management plan continued to be formulated internally even after the event, for the simple reason that as a small organisation they do not have the money to commission external consultants to do so.

However through links with trustees, the assumptions of the new plan were tested out on various member organisations, who provided informal advice, and found a few lessons for themselves as well.

They also found after the bombing that updating the plan regularly was another essential part of it. Basic information like a list of people in charge and who should take over as the decision-maker in the event that the senior members of staff are not present is extremely important. Of similar importance is the need to ensure that all members of staff have not only received a copy of the crisis management plan but have also read it and taken it in. It is not always possible to recognise how to deal with a crisis at the crucial moment, and it is not wise to rely only on the fact that you've got a good network: *"Nine times out of ten you don't need it, but on the tenth time you need it desperately."*

The Institute has been discussing the possibility of cooperation with related engineering institutions in the surrounding area. The idea that they could have sorted out some of each others problems during the crisis was not considered at the time: *"One lesson I learnt was that part of a crisis management plan was to identify friends elsewhere."*

4.5.5   HR tools

Just over half of associations, 59%, had guidelines or codes of conduct to cover relations between the organisation and their staff in the UK (based on 105 responses). The comparable figure for Ireland was 42% (based on 19 responses). All the difference can be attributed to the smaller size of the Irish associations as can be seen from the relevant section in Chapter 8.

4.6   Conclusions

One way of thinking of the professionalisation of professional associations could focus on the move from reliance on voluntary effort to use of paid staff. Most professional associations of a certain size (roughly 500 members), take on paid staff, at least part-time and generally full-time once they reach around 700 members. This is not an iron law. Two larger associations with no paid staff responded to the survey, one with 2000 and the other with 2300 members. Nevertheless, other than these two, all others above 700 had some paid staff.

This may be regarded as an indicator of professionalisation of professional associations. We think of the definition of professionalisation to mean relying on paid staff, hired for purpose, rather than 'amateur' volunteers. It is certainly easier to develop in a strategic manner if people are dedicated to the association on a full-time basis. This will clearly depend on the quality of those full-time people compared with the volunteers, whether they have the appropriate skills and experience and whether they have sufficient aptitude and enthusiasm for the work.

Certainly we believe that volunteer effort can be extremely valuable as a relatively inexpensive resource to support the management and running of professional associations. In addition by providing volunteers with opportunities to contribute, the potential gap between the organisation and its membership can be filled in, at least to some extent. The transition from complete volunteer dependency to relying more on paid staff for professional associations has been a theme pursued in several PARN publications over the past few years (Friedman and Mason, 2004a; Friedman and Williams, 2006; Williams with Woodhead, 2007).

In Friedman and Mason (2004a: 50-57) a series of case studies were presented describing cases where professional associations had moved from no full-time staff to a few. The reason why the changes were made concerned:

- A lack of consistency in effort of volunteers who were trying to provide their specialist professional services and at the same time helping to manage and run the association. There are always times, particularly for the self employed and those working in small professional services firms, when enormous extra effort is required in one's main activity and time for volunteer effort is squeezed out.

- A lack of continuity and consistency of management with changes of personnel on committees and with overlapping responsibilities among committees.

- A lack of comprehensiveness in information given to all involved due to unclear, inconsistent and unreliable communication procedures.

- A lack of appropriate match of interests and skills between what is required by the association and those willing to carry out tasks for the association. By requiring all or almost all tasks involved in the running of the association to fall on the members, who are professionals with a specialised set of skills, interests and aptitudes appropriate for their profession, inevitably, many volunteers will have to carry out tasks that they are not well suited for, or that they consider to be inappropriate for them.

These problems led to feelings among all involved of almost perpetual crisis management. Often individuals would go through a cycle of early enthusiasm and energetic contributions to the association to be followed by over-commitment and eventual disillusion and withdrawal.

Three major barriers get in the way of moving on from this situation:

- Lack of funds to hire full-time staff. In a sense the whole operating model of the professional body needs to change. Members of the club-like association run almost entirely by voluntary effort will enjoy low subscription fees and will not have to pay separately for individual member services. On the other hand the services may be of uneven quality and delivered in an amateur manner. This in itself is not an indictment and for many this is a perfectly acceptable situation. If the services are to be improved and full-time staff employed, it is likely that the subscription fees will have to rise and there may be resistance to this.

- Lack of authority to make the major change in business model described above. One of the cases in Friedman and Mason, that of the British Association of Art Therapists, made the transition through the efforts of a particular volunteer with long experience of involvement with the association in many roles. This volunteer could see the problems with the business model in place when she was elected to the position of Honorary Treasurer. This involved a 33% rise in subscription fees

- Lack of middle range foresight to construct the path towards the new model. As one interviewee said: *'We know we've got to do something, but we're not quite sure what.'* (Friedman and Mason, 2004a: 51). This may be thought of as a version of the fundamental dilemma of sustainable development described in terms of the lighthouse and torch in Chapter 3. It is clear that there is an alternative way of organising the association; most other associations are in fact in this alternative mode. However the terrain immediately ahead is unfamiliar and possibly difficult.

Possible small improvements are clear; encouraging this particular person to volunteer, encouraging that volunteer to take on a different set of tasks, communicating more by emails, changing the times of meetings to accommodate more people etc. However, just beyond the immediate terrain, there are potential potholes and barriers, which those governing the association are only vaguely aware of. For example how to deal with the issues involved in hiring staff. What skills should be looked for in the first full-time staff member? Should they for example be adept at taking over what is currently done by volunteers or should they be more concerned with coordinating volunteer effort? Should the paid staff be a member of the profession, and if not, how will current volunteers react to an 'outsider' telling them what to do and what not to do?

Nevertheless it is clear that many professional associations do successfully make the change towards organisations with substantial full-time staff, led by a chief executive with a strategic remit and eventually with a strong senior management team that also is involved in strategic thinking.

- Chapter 5 -
Income and diversification of income

5.1   Introduction

The sustainability of professional bodies is likely to depend critically on their ability to generate income from sources other than member subscriptions. Even more important for sustainability may be the generation of income from sources that are independent of the resources of the membership. In this chapter we first examine the distribution of income among the respondents, comparing the UK and Irish samples. We then look at the proportion of income from various sources, emphasising a diminishing reliance on member subscriptions, comparing the situation in 2006 with that of 2003.

5.2   Total operating income

The distribution of total operating income for the last financial year of the sample of respondents to the 2006 surveys are as shown in Table 5:1 (based on 102 responses for the UK and 19 for Ireland). The range of income was extremely wide from an income of 0 (reported by one respondent only) to over £72m in the UK and from 550 Euros (£365) to 35m Euros (£23.2m) in Ireland.

Clearly the Irish associations were on average much smaller than those in the UK with mean operating income for the sample of respondents in Ireland being 3.5m Euros (£2.3m) compared with £5.4m in the UK. Nevertheless there was a substantial proportion of Irish associations with incomes of more than £5m per year and UK ones with incomes of less than £250k per year.

Table 5:1 Distribution of total operating income: UK and Ireland[13]

Income band	Total worldwide operating income for last financial year				
	<£250k	£250-£500k	£500001-£2m	£2000001-£5m	>£5m
Frequency UK	20%	12%	22%	24%	24%
Frequency Ireland	42%	21%	26%	0%	11%

5.3   Proportion of income from member subscriptions

The range in proportions of income from member subscriptions was very wide among UK associations, from 14% to 100%. However the distribution was close to being symmetrical around the mean (average) of 52% as is indicated by Table 5:2 (the median [midpoint] was 51.5%, though the mode [most frequent] was 65%). Proportions of income from member subscriptions also varied widely among Irish associations: from 3% to 100% with a mean (average) of 56% (median [midpoint] 66% and mode [most frequent] 40%).

Tables 5:2 - 5:4 are based on cases that consistently answered questions about different sources of income (88 cases for UK and 19 cases for Ireland).

---

[13] Figures based on conversion rate as on 1 February 2007: 1 Euro = £0.6634

Table 5:2   Distribution of proportion of income from member subscriptions: UK and Ireland

	Proportion of operating income for last financial year from member subscriptions				
Proportion band	1-20%	21-40%	41-60%	61-80%	>80%
Frequency in UK	10%	27%	25%	23%	15%
Frequency in Ireland	16%	21%	10.5%	32%	21%

It is interesting that, for the UK, the proportion of associations relying on member subscriptions for more than 60% of their income was about the same as the proportion relying on this traditional source for 40% or less of their income. More Irish associations rely on member subscriptions for over 60% of their income, that is, 53% compared with 38% for UK associations. Traditionally income from subscriptions has accounted for around 80% of professional association income. Though we do not have precise figures for this estimation, it is thought to be roughly true for associations before the 1990s. In the mid-1990s Watkins et al. (1996: 22) mentioned 75% as 'fairly typical'. In both the UK and Ireland there is still a substantial minority with over 80% of their income coming from member subscriptions.

The substantial proportion of the sample reporting 40% or less of operating income coming from member subscriptions, (interestingly 37% of respondents in both the UK and Ireland) is, we believe, indicative of the future in two ways.

First, it is evidence of a 'maturing' of individual associations as they grow from volunteer managed and operated to hiring staff, and particularly staff fulfilling more control and strategic management functions. In this we propose a 'life cycle' pattern for professional associations linking growth to declining proportions of income coming from member subscriptions.

Second, it is indicative of the general professionalisation of professional associations. This requires more income in order to develop more services. It is also concerned specifically with sustainability and the outcome of risk analysis that is highly likely to lead to a strategy of income diversification. Now associations have become more sophisticated at generating income from a range of sources, thereby reducing danger of sudden adverse cash flow from a single source. Alternative income sources also reduce the need to keep raising member subscriptions when associations come to provide services that require expensive resources such as full-time staff and sophisticated IT systems and websites. This is likely to be particularly important for associations that have to compete with others for membership.

There was a slight decline in the proportion of income from member subscriptions for the 39 UK respondents who answered this question in both 2003 and 2006 surveys. The average percentage of total income coming from membership subscriptions fell from 54.6 % to 51.3% and the midpoint fell from 56% to 51%. The changes in proportions for some associations were very substantial. Five of the 39 reported the proportion of income from member subscriptions to have fallen by 20% or more. A further 15 reported falls of between 1 and 19%. Two reported no change. However, 15 reported rises of between 1 and 9% and 2 reported rises of 10% and 15% respectively.

5.4   Other sources of income

As can be seen from Table 5:3, after member subscriptions the largest single source of income for UK professional associations came from training, with examination fees and publications accounting for roughly 8.5% each. A few associations reported over 60% of income from examination fees. This table is based on the 88 associations in the UK that answered this question fully.

Table 5:3 Distribution of income by source: UK associations

Income source	Mean % of income	Distribution of associations within the range of the following income proportions:					
		0	1-20%	21-40%	41-60%	61-80%	81-100%
Member subscriptions	52.5%	0	10%	27%	25%	23%	15%
Registration/ licence fees	2.6%	72%	26%	0	2%	0	0
Examination fees	8.6%	50%	35%	9%	2%	3%	0
Training provision	13.6%	28%	46%	18%	8%	0	0
Publications	8.5%	31%	59%	6%	5%	0	0
Other	14.2%	24%	48%	21%	7%	1%	0

Table 5:4 shows that the 19 Irish associations that answered this question fully reported a similar distribution of income sources compared with the UK respondents. The main differences in distributions were the smaller proportion of income from publications and the larger proportion from registration/licence fees among the Irish associations. The publications distribution is particularly different between Ireland and the UK with 11% of associations in the UK deriving more than 20% of their income from publications and none deriving more than 20% from publications in Ireland.

The Irish in general were more similar to the UK associations in the proportion of their incomes coming from sources other than member subscriptions, which accounted for between 1% and 20% and between 21% and 40% of overall operating income. The main differences, as can be seen by comparing Tables 5:3 and 5:4, was for associations with more than 40% of income from sources other than member subscriptions. In effect, the difference is primarily in a few associations in the UK with very substantial proportions of their income coming from a source other than member subscriptions.

Table 5:4 Distribution of income by source: Irish associations

Income source	Mean % of income	Distribution of associations within the range of the following income proportions:					
		0	1-20%	21-40%	41-60%	61-80%	81-100%
Member subscriptions	55.6%	0	16%	21%	11%	32%	21
Registration/ licence fees	7.2%	63%	21%	16%	0	0	0
Examination fees	6.9%	58%	32%	11%	0	0	0
Training provision	15.0%	16%	63%	16%	5%	0	0
Publications	2.4%	47%	53%	0	0	0	0
Other	13.0%	26%	47%	16%	11%	0	0

Even though most of these income sources do not rely on member subscriptions, they still rely on member support and member resources, except possibly for publications. They all directly depend on the size of the membership base of the association. They are therefore less effective at reducing the financial risk to the association of membership falling off, than if the alternative sources of income depended on other factors. Publications can play this role, to the extent that they are bought by third parties; such as, educational institution libraries, members of connected professions and the general public.

We examined the sources of income classified as 'other' to find income sources that are genuinely independent or at least not directly dependent on member pocket books.[14] Some professional associations are sensitive to this issue and strategically set out to develop such

---

[14] Information provided in the next few paragraphs needs to be interpreted with caution. It is based on comments written into an open question where associations that ticked 'other' were asked to specify what they meant by other.

sources of income. In fact one, when specifying what the respondent meant by 'other' sources of income, stated 'income from third parties'.

Some mentioned other income from the membership such as fines and exemption applications. Clearly these fees are charged for good reason, independent of their value to the association as a source of income. However it is possible to view this source of income as a form of, or supplement to, the subscription fee that members agree to pay if appropriate as part of their joining 'contract' with the association. If viewed as a (potential) component of the subscription fee, it is clearly one that is 'charged' unequally among the membership. This is certainly appropriate in terms of the deterrence effect of the extra 'fee'. It can be dangerous for associations to rely on this as a source of income.

The source of income most commonly mentioned by UK respondents was certainly independent of membership numbers or members' resources. This was income from investments. It included interest from bank deposits and dividends from shares, and also rental of office space or room hire. However this income represented a very low percentage of the total for the few cases where the percentage was specified: only 1%-5%. Rental income was also mentioned by one of the associations in Ireland.

Another source of income, and one that seems to account for a more substantial percentage of the total for a few UK associations, is grants, presumably from the government, or possibly also from charities. Irish associations mentioned educational grants and government agency grants. One association estimated grants received to account for 23% of their income. Some mentioned donations, which may be the same as what others called grants. Donations may come from the membership (particularly into the benevolent fund), but most likely retired members or possibly from companies employing members. Donations may also include bequests.

A related source of income was sponsorship. This was mentioned by several respondents both in the UK and Ireland. This source can be problematic and some associations do not want to be associated with supplier sponsorship in any way. However, it is an income source that, if handled sensitively, can yield substantial income to associations. It may be important for associations not to appear to endorse particular suppliers, unless they have done the research and developed a robust procedure for endorsement, which is likely to be costly. If not, certain disclaimers are required as well as ensuring that there is a range of suppliers providing sponsorship. Conferences, publications and areas on websites can provide valuable sponsorship opportunities.

Advertising was another common source of income which was mentioned by several respondents in the UK and Ireland. The same media generated by the association that can be sources of sponsorship can also be vehicles to develop advertising revenue. This includes the website, journals and newsletters and stands at conferences.

Another source of revenue are various affinity deals. These may yield income to the association, or the resources may be passed on as a member benefit. However this is a source of income that is indirectly dependent on the size of the membership base.

For a few, a substantial percentage of income came from services provided to third parties for a fee. A few mentioned recruitment services. Some mentioned project work, (one UK association mentioned that their project work accounted for 33% of their income) commission income and contracts for services and consultancy. And for a few there was income from products: such as simulation sales, which was mentioned by one UK association and accreditation of health products mentioned by one in Ireland. Mostly these sources of income are derived from professional services firms associated with the profession. Income from a non-member source is an interesting subject and one that can be very important to the sustainability of the professional association. However, it can also threaten its sustainability, in that it can tie the reputation of the association to products that are vulnerable to market pressures and more open to the scrutiny of the market.

In the next chapter we examine one way of developing income from professional services firms, by allowing and encouraging professional services firms to become company members of the association itself. One organisation in Ireland mentioned under the heading of 'other' source of income, a levy scheme with independent practices.

Case study 5:1 – Income diversification
Based on an interview with Peter Coleman - Chief Executive, Association of Optometrist Ireland, February 2007.

For over 20 years, the Association of Optometrists Ireland (AOI) has been running a successful levy scheme for independent practices.

(The government refunds practice owners in Ireland for discounts on eye exams given to customers with a low income.)

There are two Government funded schemes to support the public in obtaining eye examinations and dispensing services from optometrists. The member of public must obtain prior authorisation and this is presented to the optometrist who provides service. Each month two cumulative claims are made to the Government departments for payment for these services in line with established schedules.

The levy scheme works in conjunction with this repayment: each practice owner who subscribes to the scheme agrees to pay a small proportion of the amount they can claim back to the levy scheme. The government department responsible for the refunding has cooperated with the scheme, agreeing to alter their computer system so that the levy charge is automatically deducted from the total refund and credited to the AOI.

Given the small size of the AOI, with fewer than 700 members, the levy creates a substantial amount: Although yielding less than member subscription, the system still creates around a third of the association's annual income. *"It's just a nice handy stream of income, with absolutely minimal intervention. If we stopped the scheme today, there is no doubt we would have to put up membership subscription".*

The system is voluntary, and available to any AOI member who owns an independent practice. It is primarily there to provide PR and practice support services to independent practices. A manager of a franchise for a large company, such as *Specsavers*, will pay quite a substantial overhead to the central office for PR, advertising etc. The levy system aims to provide the same kind of service for independent practices.

The AOI operate an advertising scheme in the Golden Pages (the Irish equivalent of the Yellow Pages in the UK): the AOI buys a panel displaying the association's name, and levy practice owners can then place an advertisement in that space at a subsidised cost. Members of the public find this service extremely valuable when choosing an optometrist. They see it as an assurance that practices are run by AOI members and have therefore signed up to a code of ethics and practice.

The levy system is particularly helpful for young optometrists establishing practices, for advice and contacts.

Whatever the size of the practice, the levy charge is the same percentage – less than one per cent – of the amount claimed back from the government. There is however, a cap on the levy which is often met by larger practices before the end of the year. When a practice hits the cap, the government computer will automatically stop taking money from them for the remainder of the year. This makes the system fair and ensures that bigger practices do not pay a great deal more than smaller ones for the same services.

The uptake has been very good from the outset and over 80% of independent practice owners in Ireland now participate in the scheme. Because the charge is such a small percentage spread over the year, members give willingly. There has been no pressure on the AOI from membership to cancel the scheme and as far as the Chief Executive, Peter Coleman, is aware no one has voluntarily withdrawn from the scheme.

The driving force for the AOI to establish the system was the anticipated intense competition due to the advent of British-based multiples such as *Specsavers* and Vision Express to the Irish market.

Peter offered this advice to an organisation wishing to establish such a scheme: *"It would have to be offering benefits that were perceived to be at least worth the amount of money, or else a threat that was strong enough to feel that the amount of money was worthwhile – it has to be either opportunity or a threat"*

5.4.1   Changes in the distribution of income sources between 2003 and 2006

Changes in income sources can be seen from the 39 respondents that consistently answered the distribution questions in the UK in both surveys. Interestingly of the alternative income sources to member subscriptions, one declined in the matched sample, three increased and one remained the same.

Table 5:5 Distribution of income sources: 2003 and 2006

Income source	Mean percentage of total operating income			
	UK 2003	UK 2006	Ireland 2003	Ireland 2006
Member subscriptions	54.6%	51.2%	57.7%	52.2%
Registration/ licence fees	2.0%	2.9%	4.3%	5.1%
Examination fees	8.0%	6.4%	3.0%	4.4%
Training provision	10.9%	14.4%	8.8%	18.0%
Publications	10.0%	10.0%	3.3%	2.4%
Other	14.5%	15.1%	22.9%	17.9%

- Income from member subscriptions fell from 54.6% to 51.2%

- Income from other sources that still rely primarily on member resources rose from 20.9% to 23.7%[15]

- Income from publications and other sources increased from 24.5% in 2003 to 25.1% in 2006.

In Ireland, nine respondents consistently answered the income distribution questions in both surveys. The pattern of change was similar to that of the UK associations.

- Income from member subscriptions fell from 57.7% to 52.2%, a larger fall than for the UK associations

- Income from other sources that still rely primarily on member resources rose very substantially from 16.1% to 27.5%, particularly for training provision

- Income from publications and other sources fell from 26.2% in 2003 to 20.3% in 2006.

---

[15] However this may be due to a slight change in the way this option was specified, that is, 2003 = training courses; 2006 = training provision (courses, conferences).

This represents clear evidence of movement away from reliance on member subscriptions. However it is stronger evidence for a shift towards other sources of income that rely primarily on member resources, rather than towards income that is based on third party resources. This is an aspect of association activities that we would recommend they develop strategically in future. We accept that there are complications with these income sources, as noted in the previous section and as will be discussed in the next section. Nevertheless, if done sensitively, we believe this can contribute to the sustainability of many professional associations.

5.5 Structure for alternative income generation

Many associations in the UK are constituted as charities and are restricted in what they can provide for their members. In order to maintain their charitable status, and at the same time to be able to develop diverse income streams, a number of associations (38% of the total sample in the UK) have set up commercial subsidiaries or trading arms. The same percentage of respondents did not distinguish commercial activities from other activities. Others do things in between; that is 11% have a commercial department and 14% have a commercial team or an individual dedicated to commercial activity. There are good reasons for setting up a separate commercial arm that is independent of having charitable status. As noted in Chapter 2, a professional association does not have to be formally recognised as a charity in order to have a public good remit. The public good remit is also part of Royal Charters and is often included in the objects or aims of professional associations even if they do not have charitable status or a Royal Charter. Nevertheless, it is significant that while 38% of the total sample in the UK have set up a commercial subsidiary, 64% of the sample that have charitable status (and answered the question about how they provided commercial services) had set up a commercial subsidiary.[16]

---

[16] Only one Irish respondent stated that they had charitable status and answered the question about the means of providing commercial services.

5.6 Case studies on income sources and diversification: BCS, BIFM, IEMA

The three case studies that follow provide insight into the ways that different professional associations have approached income diversification. All three of these associations are interesting in that they have approached income diversification in a strategic manner.

Case study 5:2
Based on an interview with Mike Rodd - External Relations Director, the British Computer Society, February 2007.

The British Computer Society (BCS) is a large professional and learned society with around 60000 members, 85% of whom are in the UK. They receive only about 16% of their income from membership subscription fees and the rest comes from other activities. These are mainly qualification products, which account for around 75% of their total income, publishing and other activities such as career support products. The revenue received from publishing is about £400000. For the qualification products, the BCS approach is to establish the syllabus for courses, accredit the training organisation, set and moderate the examinations, and award the certificates – above all, to control the quality of the product. The training is always delivered by an external training organisation and the BCS has over 3500 different organisations that deliver their courses.

Most of these alternative sources of income were introduced in the late 1980s, with major expansions in the late 1990s. It was a clear decision made by BCS that if they were going to be more than a small society, finding other sources of revenue was essential. Today, Mike says they are totally dependent on their income generating activities in order to survive and continue to provide member services. However he sees no alternative – certainly, as long as the BCS is serving the needs of members from a non-regulated profession so that membership is essentially optional. The extra income has allowed them to provide new and better facilities for members such as a leading-edge website, quality member publications, attractive meeting facilities, and valued career support tools - all of which attract members. BCS is unusual in having grown from 38,000 to 60,000 members in two years. However, this is at a time when there are over 500,000 IT professionals in the UK alone. The BCS needs a significant number of members in order to be a relevant body that can legitimately claim to represent the profession.

But unless they charge huge subscription fees, with increased membership comes increased pressure on the income generating activities: *"I don't know how, for a reasonably sized body, charging acceptable level fees, you can provide the sort of products that members want to see without looking for other sources of revenue."*

Admittedly, there are risks involved: *"We try to keep a fairly balanced portfolio of income generating activities, so that if one crashes, we have other sources to fall back on."*

As the Director of Publishing, Mike is pleased that they are not too financially dependent on publishing, which he believes would pose a significant risk, especially as they move into an open access environment with increased free availability of really good search tools, such as Google Scholar. He also emphasises the need for attention to the way the income-generating activities are managed; these have to be as sharply managed as in any solely commercial organisation. Thus, for example, the BCS has well-focused separate departments to do this. These income generating departments will face normal commercial challenges, for example, when it comes to competition from other bodies providing examination products.

Mike also emphasises that there is potential tension when members try to make decisions without the appropriate commercial expertise: *"In many cases you have to almost shield the members from the commercial decisions. This requires a special trusting relationship between the Trustees and the senior management team"*

Having said that, there is still a significant benefit gained from consulting members about potential sources of income, simply because they are close to the marketplace.

Case study 5:3
Based on an interview with Ian Fielder - Chief Executive, the British Institute of Facilities Management, February 2007.

The British Institute of Facilities Management (BIFM) is a not-for-profit organisation run along commercial lines. Almost half of its annual income comes from sources other than membership subscriptions. It gets 52% from member subscriptions and 48% from other sources. Amongst the other income the main sources are events, both national and regional, training, publications, and exams. It has various other small programmes which bring in some income.

The majority of these other sources were introduced in 2004 because BIFM realised then that it was too high a risk to totally depend on membership income. As a non-chartered organisation various outside influences can affect whether or not people renew their membership. With attrition rates at around 22% this was much too high to depend on fees for income any longer. The intention is to try and retain the 50:50 balance between membership fees and other sources.

The new sources of income have undoubtedly improved services for members since all extra profit gets translated into benefits, services and offers. In addition the improved services provide incentive for membership and membership grew by about 10% in 2006.

Two of BIFM's main sources of income, training and publications, were done in house until 2004 when joint ventures were introduced. They have now been turned into successful, profitable ventures. Ian Fielder, the Chief Executive, works on the basis that if there is somebody who can do something better than them this should be taken advantage of: *"My core business is membership and therefore training and publications can be done far more effectively by those who consider it to be their core business"*

BIFM finds this is a successful principle for most other things. In three years it doubled the revenue and profits of the two organisations that came together to work on training.

However in this situation, Ian Fielder emphasises the need for careful management of structure, processes and procedures to avoid any costly mistakes. There is also difficulty in managing the perception of the organisation in the market place and it is often the case that it will come under attack from other providers.

Prior to every joint venture that BIFM has undertaken, there has been a well-developed service or product already established and all it does is to add their brand and provide professional services or products: *"My advice to anybody looking at joint ventures is never develop anything. You develop them, but you don't develop them from scratch. It takes you away from your core business"*

BIFM is not entirely dependent on either membership subscriptions or the other sources for financial survival. The decision to diversify was based precisely on this desire; not to be dependent on any one source. It has a back-up plan which would reduce its own resources, staffing, and services to members if the other sources of income fell through. In joint ventures it owns the property rights, meaning that if a relationship with a partner broke down it could continue business with another partner. It also has a guaranteed financial reserve as insurance if income from any one source fails.

BIFM is looking at options for the management of its 'commercial' activities. The need for this came to light when it began publishing good practice guides, which are sponsored and sold to non-members. Those working on them are not commercial experts therefore it was necessary to bring in an external commercial manager.

In order to identify appropriate sources of income BIFM does research into what other organisations do. For example in 2006 it did a benchmarking exercise against 11 competitors in the marketplace analysing what they were doing regarding lobbying.

Ian's advice about generating other sources of income is to go to the best people in the market even if they are competitors: *"Don't be afraid of talking to your competitors, invest in research and invest in competitor analysis."*

Also communication with members about how the new income will benefit them is extremely important.

Case study 5:4
Based on an interview with Claire Draper - Director of Membership Services, the Institute of Environmental Management and Assessment, February 2007.

The Institute of Environmental Management and Assessment (IEMA) has over 10500 individual members in the UK. Between 2003 and 2006 the proportion of income they received from sources other than membership subscription fees decreased by 27%. By the end of 2006, 47% of their income came from alternative sources. They have a variety of different methods of generating this income, including training course approval, in which external training course providers approach the Institute and then pay them to quality check their courses. They also do project work in the environmental assessment field along with magazine and web-based advertising, events and conferences and publications.

The recent decrease came about due to a strategic decision to try to reduce reliance on membership subscriptions by diversifying their income over a period of three to five years. The biggest changes were in advertising which grew significantly between 2005 and 2007 and in events and conferences. The number of national events held doubled in 2006. The IEMA are now happy with the balance between membership subscription fees and other sources, but try to keep it under constant review in order to reduce risk, through their Finance and General Purpose Committee.

Through these increased sources of revenue they have been able to provide an increasingly improved service to members without increasing subscription fees. Between 2005 and 2006 they increased the number of issues of their in-house magazine provided to members from 6 to 10. They have introduced a free mentoring service for members and a free online discussion forum for specialist interest groups.

In order to manage these differing activities without a separate commercial department, they have recently undergone internal changes by creating functional teams dedicated to a certain purpose such as publications. They also contract some of the work out. Magazine and web-based advertising is done through a third party.

The IEMA ask for feedback from members, through their environmental practitioner survey and their membership satisfaction survey which goes out with membership renewals each year, about possibilities for commercial activities. However, they do not consult them directly. At the same time the senior management team keep a constant check on what other organisations are doing.

The IEMA have introduced a series of one-day workshops for members, a format which was found to work well and was replicated in other areas. Claire Draper gave this advice: *"If you find something that works, it's good to replicate it."*

- Chapter 6 -
Membership issues

6.1   Introduction

As noted in Chapters 2 and 3, professional associations are special in part because of the importance of their members. Membership of individual professionals defines most professional bodies, at least all but those that are pure regulatory bodies or pure awarding bodies. In this chapter we examine categories of members of professional associations, both different categories of individual members and the incidence and importance of organisation members. We then examine various routes to membership, and membership in relation to potential membership. Next, we deal with two particular aspects of the membership, those in the public sector and those that operate in direct fee paying relationships with clients. Finally we deal substantially with diversity issues, from the point of view of the policies of professional associations to improve the diversity of their membership and the diversity of those involved in association activities.

6.2   Overall membership

6.2.1   Membership of individuals

The average membership figure for the associations in the UK sample was 19646 (for 101 respondents) and for the Irish sample it was 2287 (for 19 respondents). The distribution of the samples distinguishing students, retired members and associates/affiliates/subscribers from fully qualified practising professionals is shown in Table 6:1 along with the percent based in the UK or Ireland.

The figures in Table 6:1 must be interpreted with caution. Some replied to the question giving numbers for the four categories of members represented in the last four rows of the table. Some replied giving percentages, even though the question asked how many individuals in the UK the organisation has for each of the four categories. There was also a problem with some leaving part of the question blank even though the question stated that if there were none in a category, a 0 should be entered. Unfortunately sometimes the numbers in the four rows added up to more than the overall number of individuals given. These cases were all rejected, which is why the sample sizes are so low.

Table 6:1 Average distribution of members by grade: UK and Ireland

| | Membership of professional associations | |
	UK	Ireland
Base	56	15
Fully qualified practicing professionals	73%	69%
Student or pre-qualified	13%	20%
Retired professionals	5%	5%
Associates/affiliates/subscribers	6%	10%

Most members of the UK respondents are based in the UK, overall for the UK sample (81 cases) it was 89% on average and for 14% of respondents, 100% of individual members were based in the UK. For Ireland, 96% on average were from Ireland (19 cases) and for 16% of respondents 100% of individual members were based in Ireland.

Table 6:1 touches on many issues of policy for professional associations, all of which require further investigation before we can interpret the figures in the table with confidence. For example, the proportion of students for the whole sample will depend on whether associations count students as members. Some associations automatically make students members of their association at no fee or at a very nominal fee. Some actively recruit students and some do not. It would be useful to compare student proportions of the membership for associations with similar policies towards students. There are also policy differences in relation to retired professionals and towards the creation of membership categories for individuals who are not fully qualified and practising. What Table 6:1 does reveal is that students are by far the biggest category of members who are not fully qualified and practising.

6.2.2   Membership of organisations

The mean number of organisation members for the UK sample was 328 (105 responses). However this mean gives a misleading impression. The majority reported having no organisation members, only 37% of the sample had any. Only 8% of the sample had organisations accounting for more than 5% of their members and in only one case did the number of organisation members exceed the number of individuals as members. For the Irish sample the mean number of organisation members was 89 (21 respondents). Forty-eight percent of the Irish sample had organisation members. At only 26% of the Irish sample did organisations account for more than 5% of the membership.

In Chapter 5 we noted the potential for income generation and income diversification of membership of organisations associated with the profession. If such organisations are small scale practices run as sole proprietorships or as partnerships among a small number of members of the profession, it seems logical for these organisations to belong to the professional body as such. How their fees are structured can be closely tied to the number of full professionals involved. These kinds of organisations are the means by which traditional professional services have been offered to the general public for centuries. However, what happens when one is dealing with huge partnerships within which there are many professionally qualified potential members that are not partners? More complexly, what about organisations that do not provide the professional service itself, but a related service or products based on the professional knowledge base and services? More commonly, there is a desire among many companies that supply the relevant professionals or the relevant professional service firms, to become as close to the profession as possible. Joining the professional association in some way, such as through affiliate status, is a very attractive proposition to them. These companies are the most common sources of sponsorship and advertising revenue for many professional associations. Where do, and where should, the professional association draw the line as to whom to allow as a member of the association? This is a subject for PARN to investigate in future.

6.3   Changes in membership in recent years

Respondents were asked how the total number of individuals as members changed in the past year, in the past 2 years and in the past 5 years.   The same question was asked about organisations as members. These results are shown for the UK and Ireland in Tables 6:2

and 6:3 based on 102 respondents in the UK and 21 in Ireland who answered all these questions.

Table 6:2 Change in individual membership in UK

	How has the total number of individuals as members changed?			
	Increased	**Decreased**	**No change**	**Don't know**
Past 12 months	68%	14%	17%	2%
Past 2 years	69%	17%	12%	3%
Past 5 years	64%	17%	11%	9%

Table 6:3 Change in individual membership in Ireland

	How has the total number of individuals as members changed?			
	Increased	**Decreased**	**No change**	**Don't know**
Past 12 months	67%	10%	14%	10%
Past 2 years	57%	24%	10%	10%
Past 5 years	67%	24%	0%	10%

Roughly two thirds of respondents in the UK reported increased membership of individuals for all three time periods. The proportion of respondents that did not know the answers to these questions was a somewhat larger proportion for the past 5 years than for the shorter period. This reflects in part the turnover of staff in associations as well as the extra effort that would be required to find out this information for the past 5 years.

Of those that responded to at least two out of three questions and did not respond 'don't know' in the UK, 63% ticked that individual membership had increased for all time periods, 10% consistently ticked that it had declined and 6% that it had not changed. This left 21% (20 respondents) who ticked a mixture.

The picture for Ireland was similar to the UK, though slightly less positive. A slightly smaller proportion of respondents in Ireland reported increased membership of individuals for all time periods. Of those that responded to at least two out of three questions and did not respond 'don't know' in Ireland, 58% ticked that individual membership had increased for all time periods, 11% consistently ticked that it had declined and 0% that it had not changed. This left 32% (6 respondents) who ticked a mixture.

Overall, individual membership in professional associations has been increasing according to the results of this survey and consistently so for the majority of associations. It is possible that there is a response bias associated with this question, that associations which have experienced declining membership may have been less likely to fill out the questionnaire than those with rising membership. However it is more likely that response rates to the overall survey were sensitive to size of association according to the number of full-time staff available to fill out the questionnaire, than growth of membership, unless the decline was precipitous.

It was regarded as too difficult for respondents to fill in by how much membership had increased or decreased. This would require further investigation.

Table 6:4 Change in organisational membership: UK

| | How has the total number of organisations as members changed? | | | |
	Increased	Decreased	No change	Don't know
Past 12 months	38%	16%	35%	11%
Past 2 years	35%	13%	36%	16%
Past 5 years	36%	9%	29%	26%

Table 6:5 Change in organisational membership: Ireland

| | How has the total number of organisations as members changed? | | | |
	Increased	Decreased	No change	Don't know
Past 12 months	50%	0%	40%	10%
Past 2 years	40%	10%	40%	10%
Past 5 years	30%	20%	40%	10%

The pattern for organisational membership was quite different from that of individual membership in the UK. Organisational membership was reported as having increased by a substantially lower percentage of associations, and a much higher proportion reported no change. Interestingly the percentage that consistently reported decreased organisational membership was roughly the same as for individual membership, 9%, and mixed at 21% was also roughly the same as for individual membership. However those that consistently reported no change were 35%, the same percentage that reported consistent increases over the three time periods. 'Don't knows' were also much higher for organisation membership changes.

The Irish pattern is different from that of the UK. There is a clear difference over the time periods that is not there for the other three tables in this section. In the past year more associations report increasing organisation members and fewer report declining organisation compared with the period over the last five years. Further investigation of whether this phenomenon is widespread (given the small base of associations, only ten respondents, represented in Table 6:5) and what has caused it is required.

6.4 Case study on organisation membership: British Institute of Facilities Management

Case study 6:1 demonstrates how easy it can be to develop organisation membership. The term used by BIFM for this type of membership was corporate, which we have changed here to organisation (except in direct quotes) in order to prevent confusion because for many associations corporate membership refers to full membership of individuals.

Case study 6:1
Based on an interview with Ian Fielder – Chief Executive Officer, the British Institute of Facilities Management.

Since its formation in 1993, the British Institute of Facilities Management (BIFM) has offered organisation membership. The institute was the result of a merger between two smaller organisations, neither of which had organisation membership. As a new organisation, BIFM realised it needed additional funds if it was to achieve its long-term objectives. Organisation membership was created with this purpose in mind.

For BIFM, it was not difficult to create interest among potential organisation members. As a conglomerate of two existing organisations, individual members who worked for large organisations were aware of the new type of membership and there was automatically a wealth of interest. BIFM did not need to do a great deal of promotion. They used media such as their magazine and the Internet to raise awareness, and relied on coverage from trade press. Ian Fielder commented, *"People were willing, and they came to us rather than us promoting it"*.

Organisation members bring to BIFM an alternative view of the industry, and have opinions which are worth listening to. As well as income, the benefits of having organisation membership are plentiful for BIFM. Organisation membership brings in all sorts of resources, for example, venues for hosting meetings. BIFM have organisation members on both the supply and demand sides, and being close to these organisations has made it easy for BIFM to keep abreast of what is going on in the industry: *"This close liaison with corporates, for us, is a very good thing"*.

In 2005, BIFM thoroughly reviewed their organisation membership structure due to the huge growth they had experienced; in 2004 they had reached 253 organisation members. Their initial scheme could not accommodate such numbers. BIFM soon realised that they were treating all their organisation members identically, as an *"amorphous mass"*. *"We realised that, although our numbers were growing, our engagement was going down, and we were actually getting less and less from our corporate members. We realised we had a problem"*.
The process of the review involved BIFM categorising their organisation members into five distinct areas:

- end user organisations (clients)

- management suppliers

- service providers

- consultants, and

- product suppliers

After speaking to representative members from each category, it became obvious that the needs and requirements for the five categories were different, and that all organisation members could not be accurately grouped together. BIFM discovered that client organisations and management organisations were very closely aligned in terms of interests. They were both very interested in providing careers for their individuals, CPD and the qualification process. Service suppliers were interested in promoting themselves, meeting clients and taking sponsorship; consultants were interested in research, innovation and speaking at conferences; and product suppliers had the very simple interest in the sales opportunities that come with being an organisation member. *"We realised that when we were treating them as an amorphous mass, the messages going out were too general and people weren't picking out what they required and needed".*

The new structure has been successful, with 23% growth in organisation members in 2005 and 20% in 2006. BIFM had to reorganise their membership department, and appoint account managers to deal with the different categories of the new structure. Organisation members have identical rights to those of individual members, bar voting rights. They are excluded from taking lead roles on standing committees, but are strongly encouraged to join the committees.

6.5   Routes to membership

A number of options were specified for possible routes to membership offered by associations. The results for both the UK and Ireland are shown in Table 6:6.

Clearly most associations offer full professional membership. In the UK, about half offer other qualifications and about half offer other forms of competency assessments. We were curious about the 20% of the sample in the UK and the 14% in Ireland that did not tick the full professional qualification box. The distribution of routes for those are also shown in Table 6:6 for the UK and Ireland. Initially we thought that those that did not tick 'full professional qualification' were those that offered the route of registration with relevant regulatory body, but the proportion of those in the UK (23%) was almost the same as the proportion of the whole sample (21%) whose membership depends on registration with a relevant regulatory body. This explanation appears to work better for Ireland 33% vs. 10%, but the numbers involved are far too small for firm conclusions.

The UK and Irish patterns were very similar. However, one difference is the higher proportion of Irish associations with reciprocal memberships with another professional body.

Some of those that ticked 'other' specified: 'working in the profession' and 'peer review' or 'experience criteria and references'. This is the traditional method of joining a profession from the times of the earliest guild-type organisations. It is relatively rare these days, but still a possible route, often in exceptional circumstances.

Table 6:6   Routes to membership

Route to membership	Percent offering route: UK	Distribution of routes for those not offering full professional qualification: UK	Percent offering route: Ireland	Distribution of routes for those not offering full professional qualification: Ireland
Full professional qualification	80%	-	86%	-
Other qualification	45%	27%	43%	33%
Other form of competency assessment	43%	50%	24%	67%
Registration with relevant regulatory body	21%	23%	10%	33%
Reciprocal membership with another professional body	15%	9%	38%	0
Interested public	18%	18%	14%	0
Other	14%	46%	0	0
Sample size	108	22	21	3

6.6 Case study on routes to membership: the Institute of Careers Guidance

Opening up routes to membership into an association that do not involve full professional qualifications can generate opposition from fully qualified members. There are good reasons for and against this practice as is demonstrated by case study 6:2.

Case study 6:2
Based on an interview with Sue Holden, Head of Professional Development, Institute of Careers Guidance.

In April 2006, the Institute of Careers Guidance (ICG) opened up full membership to those without a professional qualification. In the past, non-qualified people were offered affiliate and associate membership.

Rather than the professional qualification previously required for full membership, the new criteria are much less rigid. They are:

- to work in, or have an interest in career guidance

- to support the mission and aims of the institute, and

- to practice within the institute's code of ethical practice.

The ICG decided to make this move on the basis of what was happening in the sector, and how career guidance was evolving as a profession. Recently there has been a growth of professionals from other backgrounds getting involved with giving information, advice and guidance to young people and adults. The institute felt it was unjustly excluding many people who did not have a professional qualification in careers guidance such as teachers, social workers and youth workers, but who nevertheless worked in, and made a valuable contribution to the profession. The ICG felt that to offer these people a lower grade of membership, as was done in the past, undermined their importance to the sector: *"We felt it was time to really look at our full membership requirements and decide whether we could actually open it up to anyone within the sector, rather than putting that qualification bar in place".*

A careers advisor is normally qualified to NVQ level 4 or has a postgraduate diploma in career guidance, but there are many people

---

now working in the sector who are qualified at a lower NVQ level, but have a great deal of experience and expertise. Such people would not previously have been eligible for full membership, and the ICG felt that was an inappropriate representation of the current status of the sector, where qualification was not necessarily paramount.

The ICG felt it was important that they open up membership to different parts of the sector to recognise and react to the fact that the sector was changing. They wanted to represent the sector as it exists now in its present broad form, not as the traditional careers service which existed in the past.

A wider range of members also gives the Institute a broader base from which to respond to things and to represent their members, especially on issues such as lobbying. *"It means getting a wider breadth of opinion across the sector rather than the narrower focus that we might have perhaps retained".*

Members were involved in the change. Initially, the ICG consulted with members leading up to council meetings in 2005. As a result of this, they presented a motion at the 2005 AGM accepting the recommendations to move to this change in membership.

There were some professionally qualified members who felt quite strongly that the changes should not have gone ahead. A few people resigned or failed to renew their membership due to this change. Such members however were the minority, and the ICG believe that the move has been generally well received and that the process they went through was fair and open, giving members the chance to get involved, debate the issues and be fully aware of what was going on. *"I think ultimately we've got to a point where it's actually worked for us – we've got an increasing membership, and we've got lots of people who are expressing an interest in being part of the organisation".*

6.7 Membership in relation to potential membership of individuals

Respondents were asked if members have to belong to the organisation in order to practice. Five percent of the UK sample responded 'yes'.

Respondents in the UK were asked *"What percentage of your potential UK membership (i.e. people who meet the requirements for membership under your existing categories excluding associate/affiliate) does your organisation have?"*

This question was intended to give an indication of the degree of competition the association faces. Clearly if they have 100% of potential members in the UK, the association is protected from competition for its membership base. There was only one association in the UK and none in Ireland that claimed to have 100% of the potential membership base. However we would argue that with 90% or more of potential members, associations would have virtually no competition in that it is likely that any non-members would not belong to competing associations. This may also be said of associations with between 70% and 89%, as they would be the clearly dominant association in the field by which they define their base of potential members.

Table 6:7 shows the distribution of respondents according to proportions of potential members they believe are currently members of their associations. There were 70 responses to this question in the UK. Of these, one reported 100% to this question. As noted above, it may also be argued that the 24% of the sample that has 70% or more of the potential professional membership also have a monopolistic position. Of the Irish sample 45% have 70% or more of the potential professional membership. Overall the Irish sample of associations have a greater proportion of potential members belonging to the association compared with the UK associations. This is particularly evident in the much higher proportion of UK associations that have only a quarter or less of the potential members in their profession.

Table 6:7 Membership as a proportion of potential membership

Proportion of potential membership	% respondents: UK	% respondents: Ireland
1%-25%	50%	30%
26%-69%	26%	25%
70%-89%	14%	35%
90%-100%	10%	10%
Base	70	20

We would predict that the lower the proportion of potential membership within the association, the lower would be the proportion of income coming from member subscriptions. This is because associations that have to compete for members would be more likely to try to keep member subscriptions low, while maintaining or adding to services provided, through the development of more alternative income sources. This may be particularly important for those income sources that do not rely on the resources of the membership; that is, publications and most of the items referred to by those who specified what they meant by 'other'. Tables 6:8 and 6:9 provide evidence for this proposition.

Table 6:8 Membership as a proportion of potential membership and sources of income: UK

Sources of income	Proportion of potential membership within the associations			
	1%-25%	26%-69%	70%-89%	90%-100%
Member subscriptions	45%	61%	68%	45%
Registration/licence fees	3%	2%	2%	0
Examination fees	11%	1%	0	15%
Training provision	14%	12%	13%	19%
Member reliant but not subscription	28%	15%	15%	34%
Publications	12%	6%	3%	8%
Other	15%	19%	14%	12%
Not member reliant	27%	25%	17%	20%
Base	33	14	7	5

The hypothesis is weakly supported for the UK sample, at least for the associations up to those with 90% to 100% of potential members. From having 70-89% of potential members, through having 26-69% and 1-25%, the proportion of income from member subscriptions falls from 68% through 61% and down to 45%. Both income from member reliant but not subscription sources and income that is not member reliant rise as the proportion of potential members in the association falls. However, the prediction that the ratio of income that is not member reliant should rise even faster as the proportion of potential members falls is not bourn out. For those with 25% or less of potential members, income from sources that are mainly not member reliant is less than from those that are member reliant but non-subscription sources, while it is greater for the other bands of potential membership below 90%, and very much higher for the 26-69% group. The difference between these figures for those with 90-100% of potential members is expected; that is, that alternative income sources are much greater for member reliant than not member reliant sources.

Table 6:9 Membership as a proportion of potential membership and sources of income: Ireland

Sources of income	Proportion of potential membership within the associations			
	1%-25%	26%-69%	70%-89%	90%-100%
Member subscriptions	*54%*	*51%*	*61%*	*31%*
Registration/licence fees	7%	11%	8%	0
Examination fees	18%	3%	2%	9%
Training provision	12%	24%	12%	19%
Member reliant but not subscription	*37%*	*38%*	*22%*	*28%*
Publications	2%	1%	5%	2%
Other	7%	10%	13%	41%
Not member reliant	*9%*	*11%*	*18%*	*43%*
Base	5	5	6	2

The number of cases for each column are very small in the Irish case, however even if we combine the first two and the second two columns, we do not find a consistent relationship with the average of those with 1-69% of the potential members deriving almost the same income as those with 70-100% of potential members, 53% and 54% respectively.

6.8 Public vs. direct client relations on a fee paying basis

Respondents were asked the following questions:

What proportion of your fully qualified members work in the public sector? (i.e. government and/or publicly funded agencies)?

What proportion of your fully qualified members work in a direct relationship with clients on a fee-paying basis?

Bands were offered and the answers given to these two questions are shown in Table 6:10.

Table 6:10 Members working in public sector and members with direct fee-paying relationship with clients

% of members	in public sector: UK	in public sector: Ireland	in direct relationship with clients on fee-paying basis: UK	in direct relationship with clients on fee-paying basis: Ireland
	Proportion of sample with members working...			
1-24%	57%	67%	50%	40%
25-49%	16%	19%	14%	20%
50-74%	5%	10%	13%	5%
75-100%	23%	5%	22%	35%

This question was asked because we believed that the role that professional associations play and the services they offer are likely to be different depending on whether most of the members operate through traditional professional/client relations based on direct contact for a fee, or not. We were also aware that many associations that may be classified as in the private or public sector have members from both sectors.

The proportion with more than 50% working in the public sector and not more than 50% on fee paying basis was 28%, and those the other way round were 35% of the sample, leaving 36% of the sample with neither 50% in either of the two categories.

Comparing the distributions in the two countries, the UK sample had a higher proportion of members working in the public sector. Crudely, by weighting the proportions by the midpoints of the four bands, on average the UK sample had 36% of members in the public sector compared with 26% for the Irish sample. Conversely, the Irish sample had a higher proportion of members in direct relationship with clients on fee-paying basis. Making the same calculation the average in the Irish sample was 46% compared with the UK sample of 39%.

6.9 Diversity issues and membership

The mixture of membership of professional bodies in the UK and Ireland is changing, and arguably the potential membership mix is changing even more dramatically. Society is becoming more diverse, particularly due to rising immigration in consequence of a more general movement of people between countries in the past few decades. In addition, more people are becoming more visible as part of distinguishable groups in labour markets as representatives of these groups become more vociferous and less tolerant of labour market discrimination against themselves, and as government policy has turned more and more firmly towards clearer and more broadly based anti-discrimination by employers. In the UK distinct statutory bodies have been set up to protect particular groups: the Equal Opportunities Commission, established in 1975, the Commission for Racial Equality, established in 1976, and the Disability Rights Commission, established in 1999. These are all to be brought together in October 2007 into a single body: the Commission for Equality and Human Rights.

In consequence, the proportion of individuals entering higher education, who may be identified as coming from these groups which have been identified through government policy as the potential subjects of discrimination, has been growing. Arguably this change in membership and potential membership of the professions should not be ignored. The sustainability of the professions, and more specifically the sustainability of those organisations that currently represent the professions, will be affected by this major change. How, or what changes are likely to occur, or ought to occur is difficult to say. However there is a danger that professional associations will lose touch with substantial proportions of their membership, and particularly their student membership or potential membership, if active policies are not pursued in relation to diversity issues.

A number of questions in the 2006 survey addressed the extent to which professional associations have been pursuing policies to encourage diversity among their membership. Overall the results indicate that a substantial proportion of professional associations collect information about diversity among the membership and refer to diversity issues in their strategy document or business plan. However, far fewer have taken the next steps, to actually implement policies that encourage particular groups to join the profession and to participate fully in their professional association. For example by featuring diversity issues in member recruitment campaigns, or by organising and/or providing resources to support groups of members based on diversity issues. Diversity has several dimensions and the survey focused on age, gender, ethnicity and disability. In general a wide range of progress was found with far greater emphasis on age and gender compared with ethnicity and disability.

6.9.1   Requesting information from the membership

Table 6:11 shows the proportion of associations requesting information from the membership on a range of issues beyond the bare minimum that would be absolutely necessary to register their membership.

In the UK, a higher proportion of professional associations collected information about email addresses and professional qualifications than any of the diversity issues listed above. However only 65% asked for employment histories and 57% asked members to list their professional interests. Clearly some professional bodies ask for very little information from their members. Information on age and gender are roughly as likely to be requested as information on other issues, but information on ethnicity and particularly disability are requested by far fewer. Nevertheless the proportions requesting information on ethnicity and disability are still substantial.

Table 6:11   Information requested of the membership

Information requested concerning:	% of respondents in the UK	% of respondents in Ireland
Email addresses	94%	86%
Professional qualifications	92%	95%
Employment histories	65%	81%
Professional interests	57%	62%
Age	79%	62%
Gender	77%	43%
Ethnicity	33%	0%
Disability	22%	0%

In Ireland the picture is quite different. None of the Irish associations requested information concerning ethnicity or disability, a much lower proportion requested information about gender and a somewhat lower proportion requested information about age. On the other hand the other issues were similar except for employment histories for which clearly more Irish respondents requested information.

6.9.2   Diversity issues in strategy documents/business plans and recruitment campaigns

Collecting information on diversity issues may justify a policy on these issues, rather than being a policy in its own right. Answers to the next set of questions, shown in Table 6:12, indicate the proportion of professional bodies that actually have an active policy concerning diverse groups. The question asked was: *"Are any of the following diversity issues mentioned in your organisation's strategy document or business plan, and/or are they featured in a member recruitment campaign? (Tick all that apply)."*

The proportion of associations in the UK mentioning these diversity issues in their strategy document or business plan is substantial and the differences between the age, gender, ethnicity and disability is much less striking than for information requested of the membership.

However the order of proportions of the sample of associations referring to particular groups in strategy documents, and of being the subject of a recruitment campaign, is the same among these categories as for requests for information (with the single exception of the higher proportion mentioning disability in their strategic plan among Irish respondents).

Table 6:12 Presence in strategic plans and recruitment campaigns

Diversity Group	In strategy/ plan: UK	In strategy/ plan: Ireland	In member recruitment campaign: UK	In member recruitment campaign: Ireland
Age	25%	14%	16%	0%
Gender	21%	14%	11%	0%
Ethnicity	21%	5%	9%	0%
Disability	16%	10%	6%	0%

There was also a clear difference between inclusion in strategy or business plans and actual recruitment campaigns. For the UK far fewer have actually mounted recruitment campaigns on behalf of these groups compared with those who have mentioned them in strategy documents. Also the ratio between the two is progressively worse for the less attended to categories. Those who have mounted recruitment campaigns based on age are more than half those who mention age in their strategy document. The figures are half for gender, but less than half for ethnicity and almost as low as a third for disability. The difference between inclusion in strategy or business plans and actual recruitment campaigns was even more striking in Ireland where none of these groups featured in a member recruitment campaign for any of the respondents.

6.9.3   Recognised groups based on diversity issues

A further step towards supporting diverse groups beyond recruitment campaigns aimed at them is to support the members associations. One way of doing this is to have recognised groupings of members based on a diversity issue, and a further step would be to provide resources for such groups. Table 6:13 shows the answers to the specific question asked in the survey on these issues, which was the following: *"Does your organisation have and/or provide resources for any of the following recognised groupings of members? (e.g. women's group, young professionals network) (Tick all that apply)"*

Table 6:13 Information requested of the membership

Diversity group	Recognised grouping: UK	Recognised grouping: Ireland	Provision of resources: UK	Provision of resources: Ireland
Age	23%	19%	15%	10%
Gender	10%	5%	5%	0%
Ethnicity	9%	5%	5%	0%
Disability	6%	10%	8%	0%

The pattern here in the UK is similar to answers for the previous questions on diversity. Note the substantially higher proportion of both those having recognised groups for members by age (usually young members) and those providing resources to those groups compared with all the other categories. Unlike answers to the other questions, there was little difference between gender, ethnicity and disability for recognised groupings and for supporting them with resources. However it appears that all recognised groupings based on disability are supported by resources.

The pattern for Ireland is similar, but generally with a lower proportion having recognised groups (except for disability) and a lower proportion providing resources for these groups.

Overall we conclude that there is progress towards professional associations taking a proactive approach towards equality and diversity issues. However this progress is uneven. The proportion carrying out such policies is still small and there are far fewer addressing issues of ethnicity and disability compared with age and gender.

- Chapter 7 -
Member relations

7.1   Introduction

As noted in Chapters 2 and 6, members are vital for the sustainability of professional associations. Maintaining good relations with members is therefore important for their sustainable development. A professional attitude to member relations, involving taking care to gather member views adequately, reflecting on the services offered to members and the way they are delivered, and concern for the way member requests (and demands) are dealt with; are all critical issues.

In previous books (Friedman and Mason, 2003; Friedman and Williams, 2006) PARN has explored strategic approaches to member services and member relations. One PARN recommendation that emerged from those publications is that associations should regard member services more broadly than those that emerge from a member services department. Those are by and large goods and services that are of direct material benefit to existing members. They achieve relatively little in terms of multiple goals and long-run effects on the ecology of the professional association or the sector. Those effects providing high quality 'member services', such as the CPD programme and supports for ethical competence, are likely to have a stronger effect on the sustainability of the association. This should not be taken as an argument against providing those services that are managed through the members services department, only that they must be balanced and considered in relation to other 'member services' that are more likely to positively affect the sustainability of the association. Clearly member services are important because they deliver value to members. In addition, as noted in Chapter 5, if they generate income they can be of value both in keeping subscription fees down and in contributing to sustainability by reducing the impact of loss of member subscription income. That is, they contribute to diversity of income streams.

One mark of the professionalisation of professional associations is to develop active policies towards gathering member views. This includes developing comprehensive procedures for finding out member opinion of services they receive, as well as discovering what services members desire, and developing robust procedures for deciding which member needs and desires to satisfy. Results from the surveys on methods of gathering member opinions and the types of feedback gathered are presented in the next two sections. We examine how associations deal with complaints from members about the services they provide and who is currently responsible for conducting research on member needs and satisfaction. The second half of this chapter is concerned with critical member activities: the branch or regional network and the network of special interest groups. We conclude with some information about websites and plans for changes in member relations activities.

7.2   Methods of gathering member views

It is important for professional associations not to presume to know what their members want from them and how their members regard the quality of the services they receive. In order to assess the extent and nature of professional association efforts to gather the views of their members, the options shown in Table 7:1 were offered to respondents who were asked if the association had used any of the listed methods in the past 12 months.

For those UK associations that specified what they meant by 'other' the following were mentioned:

- Surveys at conferences of events run by particular departments

- AGM

- Online survey in membership area of website

- Telephone surveys

- Exit poll to ascertain reasons for resignation from membership

- Voluntary rates of pay survey

- Requests for comments on drafts.

Some of the methods listed as 'other' are likely to have been implied by the options offered, but not clearly enough, such as online surveys with email surveys; gathering information at the AGM with ad hoc feedback. Only 3% in the UK and none in Ireland ticked only the 'other' option.

Table 7:1 Methods for gathering member views

Method for gathering views of members	% of sample: UK	% of sample: Ireland	% of sample using only this method: UK	% of sample using only this method: Ireland
Committees or steering groups	70%	58%	3%	0
Ad hoc feedback	70%	68%	2%	16%
Email surveys	58%	47%	1%	0
Survey questionnaire to representative sample of members	53%	32%	2%	0
Survey questionnaire to all members	45%	58%	4%	11%
Focus groups	39%	47%	0	0
Other	12%	5%	3%	0

Only two Irish associations used 'other' methods, and both of them used surveys at conferences or mentioned seminars.

Most associations use informal methods and recognise that they do so to gather the views of their members. Respondents typically used several methods of gathering member views. Among UK associations only 5% use ad hoc methods or gather information through committees or steering groups, which may amount to the same thing. Among Irish associations 16% use ad hoc feedback only, and none indicated that they only gathered information through committees or steering groups.

Informal feedback may be gathered by individual members of the governing body or by paid staff at functions and conferences. Informal feedback may also come from inquiries and comments that are addressed to the association through branch coordinators, or even by whoever answers the telephone in order to tell the member that the particular request they have of the association cannot be met, or cannot be met in the manner in which the member would prefer. In addition there may be random 'orchids' or 'onions'; that is compliments or complaints about services coming in through emails or more in the past, by letter. This source of information about how members view the services provided by the association can be very important and should not be ignored. However, such views must be carefully assessed before action is taken.

As emphasised in Friedman and Williams (2006), *'he or she who shouts loudest should not necessarily get'*. The problem with using ad hoc feedback or feedback through committees and steering groups or by individual emails or letter, which are not designed specifically for gathering member opinions systematically, is that the information they convey to the association may not be representative of the overall membership. Different sections of the membership have different interests and perspectives. While those who bother to make requests or complain about services provide useful feedback, their opinions should be tested against more systematic information gathering techniques.

Roughly half the UK respondents (45%) and 58% of Irish respondents surveyed all members. Among UK respondents only 15% ticked only one of these methods and 85% ticked more than one. Comparable figures for Ireland were 26% using one of these methods and 74% more than one.

7.3   Subject types of member views gathered

Table 7:2 shows the subjects offered to respondents when asked if they had gathered views of the members in relation to a list of subjects in the past 12 months. The table compares the responses of the 86 UK associations who responded to this question and the 16 Irish associations that responded.

Table 7:2 Types of member views gathered

Types of views gathered	% sample: UK	% gathering only 1 type of view: UK	% sample: Ireland	% gathering only 1 type of view: Ireland
Ask member opinions on a particular issue	87%	27%	88%	13%
Ask members to express their level of satisfaction with existing member services	67%	0	75%	0
Ask members to express their desires for future member services	66%	0	75%	6%
Other	6%	1%	0%	0

All of the 6% who ticked 'other' in the UK survey concerned particular issues, such as CPD framework, rates of pay or local offices. A minority of respondents in both Ireland (13%) and the UK (28%) only ask for member opinion on a particular issue and conversely 81% of Irish associations and 72% of UK associations gather more than one type of view from their members. Bearing in mind the proviso that the Irish response rate is based on a small sample, it is nevertheless remarkable that a higher proportion of Irish associations are gathering the views of their members more comprehensively, in spite of the smaller size of Irish associations on average. In this sense the Irish seem to be more attuned to the importance of keeping track of member views on a range of subjects in order to maintain their sustainability.

7.4   Complaints procedures

Respondents were asked if their association has a procedure for dealing with complaints from members about the services provided by the association. Of the 107 who responded to the question in the UK, 74% indicated that they did. The comparable figure for Ireland was 71% out of the 21 that responded.

When asked to specify details, 55 UK associations responded. Of those, 20 responses were variations on the name of the system used, such as *'customer complaints system'*, *'internal online customer feedback system'*, or a description of what happens without revealing who deals with the complaints, such as *'each is reviewed, investigated and responded to on an individual basis'*, *'no specific guidelines'* or *'set out in the constitution'*. Some of the 20 misinterpreted this question and gave answers which were clearly about complaints against members of the profession such as mentioning the *'discipline committee'*. However 35 answered the question by revealing who was involved. These responses are grouped in Table 7:3 according to whether it was paid staff or volunteers and whether a staged process (more than one step to the process specified) was in place and if that process involved paid staff or volunteers.

Table 7:3 Details of procedures for dealing with complaints from members: UK

Involvement	One step	More than one step specified	Only staff	Only volunteers	Mixed
Only staff	20%	n/a	20%	n/a	n/a
Only CEO	11%	n/a	11%	n/a	n/a
Only chair of Council	6%	n/a	n/a	6%	n/a
Only Council	9%	n/a	n/a	9%	n/a
Mixture of staff and volunteers	14%	n/a	n/a	n/a	14%
Staff to CEO	n/a	11%	11%	n/a	n/a
Volunteer to volunteer	n/a	9%	n/a	9%	n/a
Staff to volunteer	n/a	20%	n/a	n/a	20%
Total	60%	40%	42%	24%	34%

It is likely that the 40% stating that there was more than one step is an underestimate, as information on the order of who deals with complaints was not explicitly asked for. Staff in 'only staff', and the first named staff in 'staff to staff', sometimes refers to senior managers, but for others it was more explicitly positions such as:

- Customer services department

- Branch Manager

- Director in charge of membership.

Often on 'staff to volunteer' it was from CEO to chairman or Council.

These arrangements are important. There are a number of issues that should be taken into account.

- Complaints by the most important group of stakeholders, members, must be taken seriously and dealt with sensitively and swiftly.

- Many members *do* have unrealistic expectations of what their association can do for them, and are upset when their expectations are not realised (Friedman and Williams, 2006: Chapter 1).

- Complaints are also a source of information on member expectations and member evaluations of the services they receive.

We suggest it is important that complaints are therefore dealt with by people who can provide explanations and possible simple redress such as an apology. It is also important for the complaints procedures to feed the issues raised into a process that may lead to more substantial changes to services provided; that is, feed into strategic management processes. Finally, it is also important that the complaints procedures do not occupy top level staff and volunteers more than is necessary.

These propositions add up to the recommendation that there be a staged process for dealing with complaints, first at a more local level and then higher up. Also that whoever deals with complaints in the first instance is well trained both in dealing with complaints sensitively, and also in following a procedure that allows the complaints to be recorded. Finally, complaints should be reflected upon and procedures are needed that will allow this information to affect strategy (though probably augmented by further information about member concerns from more comprehensive information gathering techniques as described in the previous section).

Only three of the Irish respondents provided details of the complaints procedures, and two of these merely said that the procedure was informal. The third responded that there was a formal complaints procedure. None provided the detail of who deals with complaints that would allow comparisons with the UK information in Table 7:3.

7.5 Responsibility for member relations research

Of the 101 UK respondents who answered the question, *"Who is currently responsible for conducting member needs and member satisfaction research in your association?"* most (78%) indicated an internal department or specialist and 13% indicated an external agency/consultant. Nine percent ticked 'other', and of these three mentioned volunteers such as the Council, the membership secretary or steering group (see Table 7:4). Some of these stated both internal and external and these were recoded as appropriate. One said *'staff'*, indicating that this was not a role that anyone specialised in. Others mentioned that it was done in the past or done on a casual basis. Figures for Ireland were remarkably similar to those in the UK with only slightly fewer using external agencies.

Table 7:4 Who has responsibility for research on member needs and satisfaction

Member relations research the responsibility of:	UK respondents	Irish respondents
External agency and internal department	5%	6%
Only external agency	13%	6%
Only internal department	75%	75%
Other	7%	13%
Base	101	16

Table 7:4 reveals a remarkable similarity between the UK and Irish samples.

7.6   Selected member activities

A range of traditional membership outreach activity was asked about in the context of whether this activity had changed in the past two years. Unfortunately, answers to questions on branch activities, and more so to questions on special interest group activities, were affected by a relatively high proportion of associations where the person filling out the question did not know the answers to the questions. For this reason 'don't know' and 'not applicable' responses are all shown on Tables 7:5 through to 7:8 below.

7.6.1   Branch/regional activity

Table 7:5   Changes in the last two years in relation to branch/regional attendance, activities and support: UK

Changes over the past two years in:	Increased	Decreased	No change	Don't know	Not applicable	No response
Branch/regional meeting attendance	27%	22%	26%	14%	6%	6%
Branch/regional activities	36%	16%	32%	6%	6%	6%
Supply of volunteers for branch/regional organisation	14%	31%	30%	10%	8%	7%

There is a widely expressed view that branch activity is declining among professional bodies. This is bolstered by very general pronouncements on the part of sociologists that voluntary effort is in decline, expressed as a decline in social capital (Putnam, 2000).[17] From Table 7:5 it is clear that the balance is on the one hand in favour of an increase in branch or regional **activity**, a fairly steady picture of **attendance** at branch or regional meetings and a clear preponderance of decreased **supply of volunteer effort** to support branch or regional organisation compared with increased (over two to one decreased over increased).

How should we interpret these activities? First, they demonstrate that branch or regional structures are clearly in decline in some associations, but more are increasing their branch activities and at least a similar proportion are experiencing increased attendance at branch and regional meetings than are decreasing.

From Table 7:6 it can be seen that for Irish associations the situation is on balance healthier for branches. On all these measures there were more reporting increases than decreases. As with the UK associations, there is a clear preponderance of associations experiencing an increase in branch or regional **activity** rather than a decrease (roughly five to one increased over decreased in Ireland compared with just over two to one in the UK). In Ireland there is also a strong preponderance of associations experiencing increased **attendance** at branch meetings (roughly four to one increased over decreased) compared with the fairly evenly balanced picture between increased and decreased attendance at branch meetings in the UK. The **supply of volunteer effort** to support branch organisation was fairly balanced, but slightly more reporting increases compared with decreases. This compares with a strong preponderance towards decreased supply of volunteers for branch organisation in the UK.

---

[17] Though this clearly relates to all forms of volunteering in professional associations, including willingness to stand for governance positions and willingness to support head office functions.

Table 7:6 Changes in the last two years in relation to branch/regional attendance, activities and support: Ireland

Changes over the past two years in:	Increased	Decreased	No change	Don't know	Not applicable	No response
Branch/regional meeting attendance	38%	10%	33%	0	10%	10%
Branch/regional activities	48%	10%	24%	0	10%	10%
Supply of volunteers for branch/regional organisation	24%	19%	33%	5%	10%	10%

7.6.2   Case study on regional groups

Case study 7:1
Based on an interview with a Chief Executive, February 2007.

The association (which wishes to remain anonymous) is based in Dublin and has three regional groups in Cork, Galway and Waterford. Cork was the first to be established around 30 years ago, and is the largest of the society's regional groups. The groups are quite loosely structured and do not have premises. They are managed by volunteers, with a structure consisting of a chairman, vice-chairman, secretary and treasurer.

The regional groups are funded by an annual grant of €5000 from head office which is happy to provide funding because they feel it makes them seem less of a capital city orientated organisation. Regional groups are free to allocate the funding as they like; the society only generally asks for an account of spending at the end of the year. The groups also run their own functions, which, although primarily being a member service, also generate some income towards the running of the group.

The principal function of regional groups is to provide some focus for members in particular areas. They do this essentially by running CPD programmes through the winter/ spring season, during which groups meet at least once a month. The main services provided by regional groups are CPD facilities and importantly, recognition as a local group. Recognition means that liaising with other professional bodies is made easier – there is an identifiable representative from the association in each area.

Head office chooses to have little control over regional groups. Their only restriction is that they do not make any statements on behalf of the association without first running it past head office. The Chief Executive commented, *"other than that, we leave them more or less to their own devices on the basis that they know what's good for them"*. Regional groups communicate formally with head office by having a representative on the association's council. There is however, more frequent informal communication concerning day to day issues:

> *As with any organisation based in one place, particularly in the capital, there is always the perception, rightly or wrongly among members outside of the capital, that they are not receiving the services that they consider they should receive.*

For this reason, the association has always been extremely keen to encourage these people in every way to form their own group.

The association recently increased resources to their regional groups, mainly by increasing the amount of the grants. However in addition, the society now makes DVDs of all their CPD events available to members of regional groups. CPD has always been a major factor with these groups: being a distance from Dublin, they felt deprived of opportunities. The association therefore consider these DVDs to be a major innovation.

In the past few years, there has been an increased number of the association's members outside the capital. The society are conscious that they are very much a capital city based organisation and are therefore anxious to provide whatever services they can for these members by means of increasing resources: *"We felt that by giving them funding, that this was an illustration of our commitment to them as members and as a group".*

The association believe the response from regional members has been very positive, and that it has been absolutely worth the investment.

Advice:

I certainly think that if a society can provide direct financial support to its regional groups, not to have too many restraints on it, but to operate on the basis that they are the local people, therefore generally speaking, they know what is best for themselves.

7.6.3 Special interest group (SIG) activity

Table 7:7 Changes in the last two years in relation to special interest group attendance and support: UK

Changes over past two years in:	Increased	Decreased	No change	Don't know	Not applicable	No response
SIG meeting attendance	22%	8%	23%	16%	23%	9%
Supply of volunteers for SIG organisation	15%	9%	25%	14%	26%	12%

Table 7:8 Changes in the last two years in relation to special interest group attendance and support: Ireland

Changes over past two years in:	Increased	Decreased	No change	Don't know	Not applicable	No response
SIG meeting attendance	38%	0	33%	0	10%	19%
Supply of volunteers for SIG organisation	14%	10%	38%	5%	14%	19%

Comparing Table 7:7 with Table 7:5 the proportion of 'not applicable' responses are much higher for special interest groups in the UK. That is, while 94% of the sample had branches or regional structures, only

75% had special interest groups. Also the proportion of respondents who had knowledge of whether attendance and the supply of volunteers had increased or decreased over the past two years was somewhat less concerning special interest groups, compared with branches or regional structures.

However, for those with SIGs and respondents who knew whether they were increasing, decreasing or staying the same, the picture was much healthier than for branches or regional structures. While attendance at branches or regional meetings was similar in ratio between increasing and staying the same (27% vs. 26%) and similar for special interest groups (22% vs. 23%) the proportion that experienced decreases was substantially fewer for special interest groups (only 8%) compared with decreases in attendance at branches or regional meetings (22%). Also for the supply of volunteers, increases were less than half of decreases (14% compared with 31%) for branch/regional organisation, but almost double for special interest group organisation (15% vs. 9%).

This is consistent with an overall interpretation that for professional associations as a whole, branches and regional structures are most likely to be suffering from either a withdrawal of support from the membership in terms of volunteers to help with the organisation or stagnation in support. Together these accounted for at least two thirds of associations if only respondents who knew how this support had changed over the past 2 years are considered (82 cases), then the combined figure is 82% with only 18% reporting an increase. On the other hand many, 43% of those that did know the answer and for which it was applicable recorded a growth in the activities of branches (91 cases), clearly supplied through efforts of paid staff. While this does not give a picture of overall decline in these forms of networking activities, they appear to indicate some decline of support from the membership in a substantial proportion of associations. On the other hand, attendance at meetings was recorded as increasing in 36% of those who knew and had such networks and decreasing in 29% with no change in 35% (based on 83 cases).

Overall the branch or regional structures of professional associations may be said to be fairly evenly balanced between declining and increasing, with the overwhelming proportion of associations having such a network.

The picture for special interest groups is quite different. A substantially smaller majority have such groups and those that have them seem to be less aware of them among paid staff of associations at head office. However, for those that do know about them and that have them, attendance and the supply of volunteer effort for them has been increasing in 41% and 30% of respondents and decreasing in only 16% and 19% of respondents, though it had stayed the same for 43% and 51%. The base for these figures is 58 for attendance at SIG meetings and 53 for supply of volunteers for SIG organisation.

7.6.4   Website facility

Roughly half the UK respondents (46%) have a website that enables members to update their personal details online. This represents a substantial rise from 2003. For the 59 who answered the question in both surveys, 32% said they had this facility in 2003 and 54% had it in 2006.

Only 19% of Irish respondents have a website that enables members to update their personal details online. Interestingly of the 14 who answered the question in both surveys, 21% said they had this facility in 2003 and the exact same proportion had it in 2006.

7.7   Changes in membership and/or member relations activities

As with the other sections of the survey, at the end of the membership and member relations section combined, respondents were asked if the organisation was planning to make any changes in the areas covered by questions in the section, in the next two years. Roughly half the respondents, 44%, replied 'yes'. Most of these (89%) provided comments on why they said 'yes'. They commented on a wide variety of issues. However the most commonly mentioned one (14% of them) was to do with young members; either as junior professionals or as students. Another commonly mentioned issue was to do with updating online facilities specifically to allow members to update their records themselves.

A few comments reflected the position that special interest groups are on the rise among several associations. For example one said the change *'introduced specialist certificates therefore more SIG-type groups'*, two others said it *'promoted SIGs'* and *'introduced regional meetings and special (shared) interest groups'* while another mentioned a particular SIG or sector specific group: *'we have expanded the women's group concept'*. And similarly the decline in emphasis on branches was evident, such as through regional groupings.

- Chapter 8 -
Professionalisation and sustainability by size, growth and sector

8.1   Introduction

In this chapter we examine whether certain results reported in previous chapters are correlated with certain features which may be expected to distinguish professional associations, specifically, their size (both in terms of the number of staff they employ and the numbers of members), whether they have been growing and what traditional broad sector they are in.

8.2   Size as a factor

In Chapter 4, stages in the evolution of the top paid staff member were presented reflecting two aspects of the professionalisation of professional bodies. First, the move from volunteer-managed to organisations managed by full-time staff, and second from one where full-time staff carry out primarily operational and control management functions, to one where they are employed at a strategic level and expected to participate in, and sometimes even to lead the strategic, reflective, and what we would generally call 'professional' running of professional associations. This should not imply that organisations where volunteers are more actively involved in management, and particularly strategic management of the association, are less good or less successful. It does mean, however, that the association is supported by full-time individuals, who have been recruited specifically for their skills as top-level managers, who are expected to direct the organisation in a more strategic manner.[18]

---

[18] We should point out that an alternative to hiring staff with appropriate skills and experience to bring a more strategic perspective to professional associations, would be to ensure that the volunteers involved in the governance and management have the

What we are referring to here is the well known organisational theory, that with increased size organisations must introduce more formal control mechanisms (Pugh et al., 1969). More formal organisational processes are required in order to deal with more people involved, who are less likely to know each other well enough to understand control and coordination instructions informally.

However, we must point out that the path of formalising, strategising, professionalising organisational activities, is not monotonic or unilinear, that is, it is not inevitable, it can be reversed, and it does not always progress in the same manner. As noted in Friedman and Mason (2004a: 111) the processes of professionalisation may arise from two different factors:

- growth in size of membership with attendant growth in income, and

- a change of strategy involving a new vision of how the professional association should operate.

In effect we are saying, with increasing size[19], there is a tendency towards professionalisation, but at any stage along the path of increasing size, there are choices as to how strategic or how professional to be. The changes that may be expected to occur with changes in size are not pre-programmed. They require acts of policy and may be delayed or even circumvented, if policy changes are not forthcoming.

It is difficult to separate these two factors. It has long been recognised in the private sector that there are systematic and consistent differences in organisation characteristics associated with size of organisations (see Pugh et al., 1969). Changes in organisation structure are stimulated by growth in size of organisations. There are

---

appropriate skills and experience, by very careful recruitment and particularly by training. There is little evidence of professional bodies providing serious training for top-level volunteers, beyond initial induction. This is not surprising in that volunteers are already giving their time to be present at professional body meetings and to read the papers that will be discussed at those meetings while at the same time holding down what are often full-time jobs elsewhere. This is an area for further research.

[19] Increased size may itself arise from a more strategic approach to member recruitment and retention as well as a general rise in services provided, but often may merely reflect market changes which have not been influenced by professional bodies themselves, at least in the short run.

more activities that need to be coordinated and activities that previously could have been coordinated informally or by a single person, need formal procedures for information to be elicited and for decisions to be implemented.

There are also changes in the way associations and procedures can be organised that reflect new challenges facing the professions as a whole and therefore all professional associations regardless of size. These challenges stimulate associations to become more strategic and more flexible. This can involve changes to governance, organisation structures and procedures and to member relations. However here too, a snap-shot of all associations at any one time may reveal a pattern of implementation of such changes, which relates to size. This could reflect the greater resources of larger associations that would enable them to introduce changes earlier than smaller associations. This can be compounded if early adopters of any change have to invest more than late adopters who can benefit from the experience of pioneers (sometimes in the form of products which encapsulate or support the changes which are developed after the changes have been implemented by pioneers).

On the other hand, it may be that changes depend less on resource availability or general openness to change than specific conditions in particular sectors or with particular professions, which make the challenges more acute. In this case, larger associations may be less open to change than smaller ones.

8.2.1 Size and types of professional bodies

The overall sample in the UK had roughly half of respondents (51%) that were pure professional associations and the rest were composite professional bodies, that is, professional associations with other organisations such as regulatory body, learned society, awarding body, trade union or trade association (see Chapter 3 Table 3:1), while the Irish sample was more weighted towards pure professional associations, 71%. Table 8:1 shows the size distribution (by number of staff, FT plus FTE PT) of these two types of association, pure and composite, for the UK and Ireland.

Table 8:1   Type of professional body by size (of staff)

Number of staff	UK		Ireland	
	Pure associations	Composite bodies	Pure associations	Composite bodies
0	11%	0%	13%	0
1-5	22%	12%	33%	33%
6-20	28%	19%	47%	50%
21-50	26%	28%	7%	0
> 50	13%	42%	0	17%
Base	56	41	15	6

The composite professional bodies were clearly larger on average than the pure professional associations in the UK, though the pattern was not as clear for the Irish sample. It is striking that none of the composite bodies were run entirely by voluntary effort while just over a 10% of pure professional associations are so run in both countries.

8.2.2   Size and overall regulatory frameworks

There were clear relationships between size of association (in terms of number of staff) and having a Royal Charter, charitable status and a licence to practice. The relation between size and having a Royal Charter was the strongest as seen from Table 8:2.

Table 8:2   Overall regulatory frameworks by size (of staff): UK

Overall regulatory framework	Full-time staff plus full-time equivalent part-time staff					
Staff size bands	0	1-5	6-20	21-50	>50	Total
Charitable status	0	25%	42%	50%	72%	47%
Royal Charter	0	15%	13%	27%	66%	30%
Licence to practice	0	0	0	4%	14%	5%
Base	7	20	24	26	29	106

Interestingly the really big 'step up' comes with 50 staff or more. This is particularly true for Royal Charters. Two thirds of associations with more than 50 staff had a Royal Charter but only 19% of associations with 50 staff or less had a Royal Charter. This is understandable because to achieve Royal Charter status requires having at least 5000 members.

The sample sizes are too small to take much from them, but those few associations reporting that members have to belong to the association in order to practice were all larger associations with 21 or more staff.

Table 8:3   Overall Regulatory Frameworks by size of staff: Ireland

Overall regulatory framework	Full-time staff plus full-time equivalent part-time staff				
Size bands	0	1-5	6-20	>20	Total
Charitable status	50%	29%	40%	0	33%
Royal Charter	0	0	0	50%	5%
Licence to practice	0	0	20%	50%	14%
Limited by guarantee	100%	57%	80%	50%	71%
Statutory body	0	0	0	50%	5%
Sample size	2	7	10	2	21

The Irish pattern as shown on Table 8:3 is roughly similar to the UK pattern. The proportion of associations with Royal Charters is clearly much smaller than in the UK as Ireland is a republic. Overall the proportion with charitable status is also smaller and the clear positive relation with size of association is absent. However, the smaller overall proportion of Irish associations with charitable status disappears when comparing UK and Irish associations in the same size bands. Of the 19 Irish associations with 20 or less full-time equivalent staff, 41% have charitable status, but of the 51 UK associations with 20 or less full-time equivalent staff, 15 or 29% have charitable status. Comparable figures for this size group for licence to practice are 11% for Ireland and only 2% for the UK.

The two alternative options offered to the Irish respondents ('limited by guarantee' and 'statutory body') gave inconclusive results in terms of correlations with size of association.

8.2.3   Size and financial management tools

As can be seen from Table 8:4 there was a strong relation between the financial management tools and size of association in the UK. The relationship was clearest and most consistent when size of association is measured by number of staff employed.

Table 8:4   Financial management tools by size of staff: UK

Financial management tool	Full-time staff plus full-time equivalent part-time staff					
Size bands	0	1-5	6-20	21-50	>50	Total
Business plans	67%	92%	79%	96%	100%	91%
Risk management	17%	15%	50%	72%	82%	58%
Internal audit	50%	39%	38%	48%	75%	52%
Sample size	6	13	24	25	28	96

The proportions are most consistently and strongly associated with size for risk management. The relationship was least strong for internal audit. There is an interesting distinction between the three size levels above 5 full-time equivalent employees and the smaller ones. The three size levels above 5 full-time equivalent staff members are completely consistent in their relationship between each of the financial management tools and staff size. However the two smaller sizes are not completely consistent with the rest or with each other in terms of a positive relation between use of these tools and size.

We would regard the 18 UK respondents with 5 or less full-time equivalent staff as basically run by volunteers either with no paid staff support or with very limited support. (We note that of these 18 respondents, 5 had no full-time staff and 5 had only 1 full-time staff member). Interestingly associations with no paid staff resources at their disposal were more likely to control their finances using internal audit than those with substantial full-time staff (though the sample size is very small). Volunteer-run audit committees seem to be important for associations without staff.

On the other hand, risk management seems to be an activity undertaken primarily by paid staff, or supported by paid staff. This may be a problem for small associations as undertaking risk assessment and risk management is highly recommended by the Charity Commission for governing bodies. It is actually a measure of how far the professionalisation of professional associations has yet to go that only 58% of respondents in the UK, 15% in Ireland have risk management systems. However as noted in Chapter 4, the use of both internal audit and risk management tools has increased between 2003 and 2006 among those associations that responded to both surveys. Table 8:5 shows that the relation between size and use of business plans, risk management and internal audit holds for Ireland as well, though the pattern is less strong due primarily to smaller sample size. Formal external audit does not appear to be associated with size.

Table 8:5   Financial management tools by size of staff: Ireland

Financial management tool	Full-time staff plus full-time equivalent part-time staff				
Size bands	0	1-5	6-20	>20	Total
Business plans	50%	50%	50%	100%	55%
Risk management	0	0	20%	50%	15%
Internal audit	0	17%	50%	100%	40%
Formal external audit	100%	83%	80%	100%	85%
Sample size	2	6	10	2	20

8.2.4   Size and employee relations tools

It is not surprising that use of employee relations tools would be directly correlated with size of association staff. The relationship was particularly clear cut among Irish associations (Tables 8:6 and 8:7), though the sample size is small. While a lower proportion of Irish respondents have guidelines or codes of conduct to cover relations between the organisation and their staff compared with the UK, the proportions are less divergent for similarly sized associations; that is for associations with 20 or less full-time equivalent staff, the proportions are 38% for Ireland and 40% for the UK.

Table 8:6 Guidelines for staff relations by size of staff: UK

	Number of full-time staff plus full-time equivalent part-time staff					
	0	**1-5**	**6-20**	**21-50**	**>50**	**Total**
% respondents having guidelines or code	0	40%	50%	73%	79%	59%
Sample size	6	20	24	26	29	105

Table 8:7 Guidelines for staff relations by size of staff: Ireland

	Number of full-time staff plus full-time equivalent part-time staff				
	0	**1-5**	**6-20**	**>20**	**Total**
% respondents having guidelines or code	0	17%	50%	100%	42%
Sample size	0	6	10	2	19

8.2.5 Size and income sources distribution

Table 8:8 shows that the proportion of income derived from member subscriptions generally declines with the size of associations for the UK sample. Income not from subscriptions but from member resources (registration, examination, training) rises strongly with size, while the pattern for non-member resource income streams (publications, other) is less clearly related to size of associations.

Table 8:8 Sources of income by size (of membership): UK

Sources of income	Number of individual members				
	1-500	501-1500	1501-5000	5001-20000	>20000
Membership subscriptions	67%	62%	55%	40%	49%
Registration/licence fees	0	1%	5%	2%	3%
Examination fees	0	3%	7%	9%	15%
Training provision	13%	17%	13%	17%	9%
Publications	14%	7%	5%	13%	9%
Other	7%	11%	14%	19%	15%
Sample size	4	11	24	20	20

Table 8:9 for Ireland shows a similar pattern to the UK, but less clear-cut in relation to size. This is in part due to the small sample size.

Table 8:9 Sources of income by size (of membership): Ireland

Sources of income	Number of individual members			
	1-500	501-1500	1501-5000	>5000
Membership subscriptions	40%	77%	51%	44%
Registration/licence fees	17%	0	4%	13%
Examination fees	0	0	15%	20%
Training provision	26%	13%	16%	9%
Publications	1%	3%	4%	0
Other	16%	8%	11%	14%
Sample size	3	7	6	2

8.2.6 Size and categories of individual membership

The distribution of the sample by categories of individual membership according to size by number of individual members is shown in Table 8:10.

Table 8:10 Categories of membership by size (of membership): UK

Membership band	Membership of professional associations					
	1-500	501-1500	1501-5000	5001-20000	>20000	Total sample
Sample size	6	10	16	13	11	56
% based in the UK	98%	94%	96%	89%	85%	92%
% fully qualified practicing professionals	81%	87%	77%	66%	59%	73%
% student or pre-qualified	5%	5%	12%	12%	27%	13%
% retired professionals	4%	4%	6%	5%	5%	5%
% associates/ affiliates/ subscribers	11%	4%	4%	10%	3%	6%

Table 8:10 reveals that, for the UK sample, the larger the association, the more likely that the percentage of fully qualified practicing professionals will be lower and that the percentage of student or pre-qualified members will be higher. The proportion of retired does not appear to be sensitive to the size of the association measured by the number of individual members, nor does the proportion of associates/affiliates/subscribers.

Table 8:11   Categories of membership by size (of membership): Ireland

Membership band	Membership of professional associations				
	1-500	501-1500	1501-5000	>5000	Total sample
Sample size	3	5	6	1	15
Based in Ireland	97%	96%	96%	99%	96%
Fully qualified practicing professionals	61%	79%	69%	43%	69%
Student or pre-qualified	10%	13%	25%	51%	20%
Retired professionals	6%	9%	2%	0%	5%
Associates/ affiliates/subscribers	27%	4%	8%	0%	10%

Table 8:11 for Ireland shows a similar relationship between rising student or pre-qualified proportions of the membership for larger associations. However the proportion of student or pre-qualified is generally lower than in the UK for the majority in the 501-1500 and the 1501-5000 member categories.

8.2.7   Size and member relations through branch and SIG networks

The branch figures in Table 8:12 are based on 77 cases and the SIG figures on 53 cases. There was a consistent relation between size of association and the proportion of associations reporting increased branch/regional meeting attendance. However there was not a consistent negative relation between size and those that reported declining attendance. There was a consistent negative relation between size and those that reported no change in attendance.

The relationship between size and attendance at SIG meetings was less clear. Very roughly a smaller proportion of the larger associations reported declining attendance at SIG meetings.

Table 8:12   Changes in branch/regional and SIG attendance by size (of membership): UK

		Number of individual members				
		1-500	501-1500	1501 - 5000	5001-20000	>20000
Branch/ regional meeting attendance	Increased	25%	30%	32%	37%	47%
	Decreased	0	30%	32%	37%	26%
	No change	75%	40%	36%	26%	26%
SIG meeting attendance	Increased	0	57%	25%	62%	47%
	Decreased	25%	29%	8%	15%	6%
	No change	75%	14%	67%	23%	47%

Table 8:13 is based on 75 cases for branch/regional organisation and 47 cases for SIGS. The supply of volunteers for branches and regional organisation does seem to be somewhat related to the size of the association, with larger associations having more success than smaller ones, except for the very smallest associations. There does not appear to be a clear relation between size of association and the direction of change in the supply of volunteers for SIGS.

Table 8:13   Changes   in   supply   of   volunteers   for branch/regional and SIG organisation by size (of membership): UK

		Number of individual members				
		1-500	501-1500	1501 - 5000	5001-20000	>20000
Supply of volunteers for Branch/ regional organisation	Increased	25%	0	8%	22%	35%
	Decreased	50%	63%	32%	56%	30%
	No change	25%	38%	60%	22%	35%
Supply of volunteers for SIG organisation	Increased	50%	33%	15%	54%	27%
	Decreased	0	33%	8%	27%	13%
	No change	50%	33%	77%	18%	60%

Table 8:14 shows the distribution of responses by size of association to the question of whether branch/regional activities have changed. It is based on 83 responses. The table shows a clear correlation between size of associations and the balance of proportions reporting increased activities compared with decreased activities. For the smallest size band the proportion of those reporting increased activities is the same as those reporting decreased activities. The ratio of increase over decrease rises from 1:1 to roughly 1.5:1 for the next three size bands and for the highest size band the ratio is 12:1.

Table 8:14   Changes in branch/regional activities by size (of membership): UK

Branch/regional activities	Number of individual members				
	1-500	501-1500	1501 - 5000	5001-20000	> 20000
Increased	25%	50%	28%	46%	60%
Decreased	25%	30%	20%	25%	5%
No change	50%	20%	52%	29%	35%

8.3   Growth as a factor

As shown in Chapter 6 (Tables 6:2 and 6:3), most respondents reported growth in membership over three time periods: the past 12 months, the past 2 years and the past 5 years. Considering only the 100 in the UK that responded either increase, decrease or no change for at least two of the three time periods (that is, 1 'don't know' response at most), we created a variable to examine the relation between growth of associations and responses to other questions as follows:

- Consistent increase – associations indicating that their membership had increased in all three time periods: (59%)

- Overall decrease – associations indicating that their membership had decreased in all three time periods (9) plus associations that reported a combination of no change and decrease (7): 16%.

- Overall no change/mixed - associations indicating that their membership had not changed in all three time periods (6) plus associations that reported no change in any 2 of the 3 time periods, increase in any 2 or the 3 time periods, or a combination of increase, no change and decrease (19): 25%.

We weighted this measure (by restricting the 'consistent increase' more strictly than the 'overall decrease' categories) in order to try to get more equal proportions of the sample in each of the three categories.[20]

8.3.1   Growth and type of professional body

Table 8:15 compares pure professional associations and composite professional bodies by growth of membership. In the UK there is little difference. The majority of both types of organisations seem to be enjoying consistent increases in membership. The picture in Ireland is slightly different with pure associations doing somewhat better than the composite bodies.

---

[20] It is possible that there has been some bias in response rates, with those that had been consistently increasing being more likely to respond to the survey, in part due to them being more able to spare resources to complete the questionnaire.

Table 8:15 Type of professional body by membership growth

	UK		Ireland	
	Pure associations	**Composite bodies**	**Pure associations**	**Composite bodies**
Consistent increase	57%	59%	62%	50%
Overall decrease	16%	17%	15%	33%
Overall no change/ mixed	27%	24%	23%	17%
Base	49	41	13	6

8.3.2   Growth and financial management tools

Table 8:16 provides information on use of financial management tools comparing associations experiencing consistent growth with those reporting overall decline or a mixed change.

Table 8:16 Financial management tools by membership growth: UK

Financial management tool	**Growing and declining membership**			
	Consistent increase	**Overall decrease**	**Overall no change/mixed**	**Total**
Business plans	91%	75%	100%	91%
Risk management	66%	58%	36%	58%
Internal audit	57%	58%	46%	54%
Sample size	56	12	22	90

Interestingly those which have consistently increased and decreased overall were more likely to be undertaking risk management and internal audit than the mixed cases. The opposite was the case for business plans.

**Table 8:17   Financial management tools by membership growth:
Ireland**

Financial management tool	Growing and declining membership			
	Consistent increase	Overall decrease	Consistent increase	Total
Business plans	64%	75%	0	56%
Risk management	27%	0	0	17%
Internal audit	46%	25%	0	33%
Sample size	11	4	3	18

Table 8:17 shows the position for Ireland. This table is not conclusive due to the small sample size in Ireland in the overall decrease and overall no change/mixed categories. However there seems to be some consistency in the risk management figures with over a quarter of associations that have experienced consistent membership growth using this tool. Arguably these have more to lose if risks materialise following the adage: 'the bigger you are the harder you fall'. However it is more likely that those showing consistent growth are more likely to be able to afford the resources required to carry out risk analysis, that is, they are less likely to be caught up in fire-fighting. Nevertheless to turn declining membership around, something like risk management systems as part of general sustainability analysis (as described in Chapter 3) is urgently required.

8.3.3   Growth and member relations through branch and SIG networks

The branch attendance figures for the UK in Table 8:18 are based on 76 cases and the SIG attendance figures on 55 cases. As would be expected, there was a clear correlation between growth of individual membership and proportions reporting an increase in attendance in both branch and SIG meetings. Conversely there was also a correlation between decline in membership and proportions reporting a decrease in attendance in both branch and SIG meetings. It is interesting that these correlations are stronger for SIG attendance than for branch attendance.

Table 8:18 Changes in branch/regional and SIG attendance by growth in membership: UK

		Growth in individual membership		
		Consistent increase	Overall decrease	Overall no change/ mixed
Branch/ regional meeting attendance	Increased	44%	20%	30%
	Decreased	22%	60%	35%
	No change	35%	20%	35%
SIG meeting attendance	Increased	53%	13%	40%
	Decreased	6%	38%	20%
	No change	41%	50%	40%

Table 8:19 is based on 76 cases for supply of volunteers for branch/regional organisation, and 51 cases for SIG organisation. As can be expected, associations experiencing consistent increases are more likely to have increased supplies of volunteers for both branch and SIG organisation compared with those with no change or mixed changes and particularly compared with those experiencing overall decreases in membership. This is borne out in the table.

Clearly the causality primarily runs from growing membership to increased supply of volunteers for outreach and networking activities at the association. However, it may also run in the opposite direction too, that is, if the supply of volunteers dries up for supporting the association's networks, this may be a sign of deterioration in support for the association itself that may in turn impact on recruitment and retention of members.

Table 8:19 Changes in supply of volunteers for branch/regional and SIG organisation by growth in membership: UK

		Growth in individual membership		
		Consistent increase	Overall decrease	Overall no change/ mixed
Supply of volunteers for branch/ regional organisation	Increased	29%	8%	6%
	Decreased	31%	69%	50%
	No change	40%	23%	44%
Supply of volunteers for SIG organisation	Increased	29%	20%	40%
	Decreased	16%	40%	20%
	No change	55%	40%	40%

Members are critical for the sustainability of professional associations, but those members who volunteer to help keep the association going, and particularly those involved at local levels, are especially important.

Table 8:20 compares change in branch/regional activities according to growth of individual membership. It is based on 84 responses.

Table 8:20 Changes in branch/regional activities by growth in membership: UK

Branch/regional activities	Growth in individual membership		
	Consistent increase	Overall decrease	Overall no change/mixed
Increased	48%	15%	48%
Decreased	12%	46%	19%
No change	40%	39%	33%

While there was little difference between change in branch/regional activities for associations experiencing consistent increase in individual membership and those which are experiencing no change or a mixed pattern of membership change, there was a strong difference between that pattern and that of associations experiencing an overall decrease in membership. Again, it is likely that the primary direction of causality is from change in membership to change in branch regional activities.

More resources coming into the association make it easier for branch/regional activities to be funded and more people coming into the association makes it more likely that such activities will be well attended. However, the reverse causality may also operate with an upward spiral of rising membership leading to rising vitality of the branch/regional network *and* rising branch/regional activities, in turn, helping to recruit more members. This process can be regarded as an example of the third strategy or process of stimulating sustainability (described in Chapter 3) which is based on time-dependent interactions between the association and an aspect of its ecology. In this instance the ecological factor is both the current members of the association and potential members.

8.4   Sector as a factor

Traditional sectors are problematic in relation to professional bodies. On one hand certain professional bodies have a clear idea of what sector they are in and exercise that understanding by benchmarking exclusively against other professional bodies in 'their' sector. Also some associations have joined to form umbrella groups to strengthen the power of their voice as representatives of professionals in those sectors. In part this reflects the way government departments are organised, due to the importance of government lobbying.

Many times members of associations have told PARN that the sector breakdown is difficult to get right because many associations straddle traditional sector divisions.   This is because the sector divisions themselves are artefacts of government census policies and the history of those policies, and because associations change the distribution of their membership across these sectors due to changing policies and merger activity. Furthermore they say that the key differences have more to do with whether professions are licensed or not and whether the association must attract members either from other associations or from the position of not belonging to any association. The latter associations have greater pressure on them to provide members with good value services for the subscription fees, though this pressure is not absent even for licensed professions.

The make up of the four (sub)sectors that we use in the section below is given in Chapter 1 (Table 1:2).

8.4.1 Sector by type of professional body

Table 8:21 compares pure professional associations and composite bodies of professional associations with other types of organisations by sector. In both the UK and Ireland the 'health and social' sector has the highest proportion of composite bodies, and this is particularly so for the Irish sample. Overall the Irish sample was composed of a higher proportion of pure professional associations than the UK sample.

Table 8:21   Type of professional body by sector

	UK		Ireland	
	Pure associations	Composite bodies	Pure associations	Composite bodies
Health & social	48%	52%	33%	67%
Finance, law, business, management	69%	31%	71%	29%
Engineering, science, environment, construction	54%	46%	86%	14%
Education, media, culture	62%	39%	100%	0
Overall	58%	42%	74%	26%
Base	56	41	14	5

8.4.2 Sector and financial management tools

Sectors did not provide much difference in the use of financial management tools. The four sectors ranged only between 48% and 55% for internal audit, 86% and 100% for business plans and 50% and 60% for risk management. Business sector associations had the highest frequency for use of business plans and risk management and lowest for internal audit.

8.4.3 Sector and distribution of income sources

Table 8:22 shows that 'education, media and culture' is the sector most reliant on member subscriptions, while 'finance, law, business and management' was the least. The prime reason for this difference is the relatively high proportion of income coming from registration/licence fees for associations in the 'finance, law, business and management' sector.

Table 8:22 Income sources by sector: UK

Income source	Sector			
	Health & social	Finance, law, business, management	Engineering, science, environment, construction	Education, media, culture
Member subscriptions	53%	46%	53%	59%
Registration/ licence fees	3%	4%	2%	0%
Examination fees	7%	17%	4%	7%
Training provision	10%	17%	13%	15%
Publications	6%	8%	12%	8%
Other	20%	8%	16%	12%
Sample size	22	24	29	11

Even though the 'health and social', and the 'engineering, science, environment and construction' sectors did not stand out in terms of a low proportion of income from member subscriptions, they did stand out in having a high proportion of income from sources which do not rely on member resources (publications and other).

8.4.4   Sector and member relations through branch and SIG networks

Table 8:23   Changes in branch/regional and SIG attendance by sector: UK

		Sector			
		Health & social	Finance, law, business, management	Engineering, science, environment, construction	Education, media, culture
Branch/ regional meeting attendance	Increased	33%	45%	35%	27%
	Decreased	40%	28%	27%	27%
	No change	27%	28%	39%	45%
SIG meeting attendance	Increased	47%	69%	32%	11%
	Decreased	20%	0	16%	33%
	No change	33%	31%	53%	56%

The branch figures in Table 8:23 are based on 81 cases and the SIG figures on 56 cases. This reflects the numbers that had branches or SIGs and that could say whether attendance at them had changed. From the table it is clear that both the branch network and especially the SIG network are growing most commonly among associations in the 'finance, law, business and management' sectors. The branch network is more commonly declining in the 'health and social' sector and the SIG network more commonly declining in the 'education, media and culture' sector.

Table 8:24 Changes in supply of volunteers for branch/regional and SIG organisation by sector: UK

		Sector			
		Health & social	Finance, law, business, management	Engineering, science, environment, construction	Education, media, culture
Supply of volunteers for branch/ regional organisation	Increased	12%	32%	15%	8%
	Decreased	59%	36%	39%	33%
	No change	29%	32%	46%	58%
Supply of volunteers for SIG organisation	Increased	33%	54%	24%	0
	Decreased	25%	8%	18%	33%
	No change	42%	39%	59%	67%

As Table 8:24 shows, change in the supply of volunteers overall is healthiest in the 'finance, law, business and management' sector. It is not very healthy in 'education, media and culture'. The other two sectors are mixed with a balance in favour of decreases in supply of volunteers for branch/regional organisation and a balance in favour of increases in supply of volunteers for SIG organisation. This difference was particularly pronounced in the 'health and social' sector.

Table 8:25 compares change in branch/regional activities according to sector and is based on 89 responses.

Table 8:25 Changes in branch/regional activities by sector: UK

Branch/ regional activities	Sector			
	Health & social	Finance, law, business, management	Engineering, science, environment, construction	Education, media, culture
Increased	50%	54%	36%	23%
Decreased	25%	11%	21%	23%
No change	25%	36%	43%	54%

The 'health and social' sector is interesting in that a high proportion of respondents reported increased activities in their branch/regional network, but a lower proportion reported increased attendance at branch/regional meetings and a much lower proportion reported increased supply of volunteers for branch/regional organisation. This would suggest that associations in this sector are attempting to revitalise their branch/regional networks. It will be interesting to see if this leads to changes in attendance and volunteer support in future.

8.5 Conclusions

8.5.1 Size

Overall the composite professional bodies were larger than the pure professional associations, taking the number of full-time plus full-time equivalent part-time employees as the measure of size. We may regard this as indicating a development pattern for professional associations, that is, as they develop and grow, they take on other roles associated with different professional bodies. However while this may be a pattern common to some that become awarding bodies and learned societies in addition to professional associations, it is unlikely that regulatory functions will be associated with professional association development. This is a subject requiring further research.

There was a strong correlation between size of associations and both charitable status and achieving a Royal Charter. These characteristics, and particularly that of achieving a Royal Charter, are clearly marks of more mature and well established associations.

There was a clear link between size of association and taking on financial management tools, especially risk management and also guidelines on relations between the organisation and its employees. These may be regarded as evidence of the professionalisation of professional associations.

There was also a positive relation between size of association and consistent increases in branch attendance, supply of volunteers to support branch organisation and especially with branch activities. It is interesting that the positive relation between size and robust growth in the SIG network did not apply.

8.5.2   Growth

It seems to be a contradiction, but associations that are consistently increasing as well as those which are decreasing overall, were more likely to be undertaking risk management and internal audit than thse with mixed growth or no change. The opposite was the case for business plans. However those consistently increasing were more likely to be using all of these financial management tools than those experiencing overall decreases in membership. There are several ways of interpreting these results. Is it that associations that least need these tools are most likely to be using them? Is it that use of these tools has helped associations to grow consistently?   Is it just that associations that are characterised with a more professional or strategic management are more likely both to be using these tools and more likely to be growing?

There is a similarly interesting connection between growth of membership and both growth in branch networks and in SIG networks. This applies to the supply of volunteers, attendance and branch activities. We believe the causality primarily runs from growing membership to increased supply of volunteers for outreach and networking activities at the association. We accept that the causality may also run in the opposite direction. Declining supply of volunteers to support networks may signal overall deterioration in support for the association, which may in turn impact on recruitment and retention of members.

8.5.3   Sector

We did not find that the sector breakdown that we used was particularly clear in defining different answers to the questions posed in the survey. However the 'finance, law, business and management' sector did consistently show the most robust branch and SIG networks among the four sectors.

- Chapter 9 -
Conclusions and
recommendations

9.1   Introduction

In this chapter we briefly return to the three broad themes outlined in Chapter 1 for this book.

9.2   Conclusions   about   the professionalisation   of   professional associations

In Chapters 4 and 8 we provided substantial evidence for the professionalisation of professional associations to be associated with their size. To some extent it is a natural consequence of increasing size of organisations that they become more formal. Formality can sometimes be mistaken for professionalisation, for a more strategic approach to management, because the ways in which strategic thinking occurs are more explicit. Nevertheless we suspect that there is a real correlation between size and a more professional approach to managing professional associations.

This is particularly so when professional associations put themselves under the regulatory frameworks associated with charitable status and Royal Charters.

In general the Irish associations showed less evidence of professionalisation than the UK sample, but much of this was due to size. In the case of guidelines to cover relations between the organisation and its staff, the difference seems entirely due to size rather than country, in the case of risk management and internal audit systems it is a function of both size and country.

Also there are some aspects of Irish associations that may be taken as more evident 'professionalism' than for associations in the UK, such as in gathering member views using all member surveys.

9.3 Conclusions and recommendations about the sustainable development of professional associations

In Chapter 3 we introduced the idea of applying sustainability concepts and particular strategies for achieving sustainability to professional associations. Three broad strategies were discerned. The first, risk assessment and risk management, is focused on avoiding certain actions, or taking actions that will nullify or alleviate harmful situations. They are in this sense prophylactic, designed to protect the association, based on the anticipation of negative situations that may be avoided, or countered, or the impact of which may be reduced through vigilance.

The other two strategies we discern are more positive and proactive. These are to direct policies and activities towards achieving multiple goals at the same time and to focus on policies and activities that have lingering effects on the ecology of associations, their members, the profession as a whole and the sector of professional associations as a whole.

In this book we have asked about risk management directly and investigated diversification of income as a major way of mitigating risk. Strategies that involve multiple goals and long term effects have only been touched on here in relation to the development of the branch and SIG networks, and those primarily affect members and aim at satisfying their material, social and professional needs. Rather we have used this opportunity to begin a discussion about sustainability and professional associations.

The following set of recommendations are based on the material presented in Chapter 2. It is not comprehensive, due in part to the unfinished nature of the concept of sustainable development, and in part to our recent interest in the concept.

- Find an area of expertise concerning professionalism and professionalisation of professional associations and develop a reputation for it.

- Be a pioneer at certain things.

- Be a close follower of pioneers, but one who reflects on pioneer experiences in order to develop something that takes advantage of those experiences.

- Diversify income streams to meet income risk and in particular consider the development of income streams that do not rely on member resources.

- Deal with other risks strategically through careful and frequent risk assessment exercises and the development of robust risk management systems. These should include crisis management plans.

- Analyse stakeholders and aims, and develop strategic plans based on these categories.

- Consider the links among stakeholders and analyse the links among your aims and see if you can develop activities that stimulate those links positively or that take advantage of those links.

- Carry out a multiple goal analysis to identify activities that service multiple goals and assign special multiple goal management and monitoring staff or create events where this issue is discussed.

- Carry out a time-dependent ecological effects analysis to identify activities that have long term substantial effects on the ecology of the association and assign special management and monitoring staff or create events when this issue is discussed.

9.4   Conclusions about the professional associations sector

Professional associations do not yet regard themselves as a sector, first and foremost. To do so will require the processes by which the professions have come under pressure from clients, the government and the media to continue and possibly to become even more severe in future. One way of hastening this process, which we believe will encourage them all to improve, to the benefit of clients and the general public as well as the membership and potential membership of these associations, will be for governments and major employers to recognise their contribution to society and the economy.

Currently there is no government agency in the UK or Ireland that recognises and supports the professions for the important role they play in the economy and society. This is a serious lacuna. In the UK different government departments deal with different professions, primarily with the purpose of regulating them. The government department in the UK that is charged with supporting aspects of the economy is the Department for Trade and Industry (DTI) but at the DTI the professions hardly figure in their own right.

PARN will continue to develop publications and events that throw a light on the professional associations as a sector with the aim of encouraging them to learn from each other and to develop practices that are sustainable and robust.

Bibliography

Bibliography

Abbott A. (1988). The System of the Professions, Chicago: University of Chicago Press.

Anheier, H.K. (2000). *Managing Non-profit Organisations: Towards a New Approach*, Civil Society Working Paper 1, January.

Charity Commission (2003) CC22 - *Choosing and Preparing a Governing Document* http://www.charity-commission.gov.uk/publications/cc22.asp#33

Charity Commission http://www.charity-commission.gov.uk/spr/corcom1.asp

Drucker, P. (1990). *Managing the Non-Profit Organisation: Principles and Practices*, New York: Harper Collins.

Fama E. and Jensen M. (1983). 'Separation of ownership and control', *Journal of Law and Economics*, 26: 301-325.

Freeman, R. E. (1984). *Strategic Management: A Stakeholder Approach*, Boston: Pitman Publishing.

Friedman A. (ed) (2005). *Critical Issues in CPD*, Bristol: PARN.

Friedman A., Daly S. and Andrzejewska R. (2005). *Analysing Ethical Codes of UK Professional Bodies*, Bristol: PARN.

Friedman A.L., Davis K., Durkin C. and Phillips M. (2000). *Continuing Professional Development in the UK: Policies and Programmes,* Bristol: PARN.

Friedman A. and Mason J. (2003). *Analysing Member Services: A Strategic Perspective for Professional Associations*, Bristol: PARN.

Friedman A. and Mason J. (2004a). *The Professionalisation of UK Professional Associations: Governance, Management and Member Relations,* Bristol: PARN.

Friedman A. and Mason J. (2004b). *Professional Associations in Ireland: A Comparative Study with the UK,* Bristol: PARN.

Friedman A.L. and Mason J. (2006). *Governance of Professional Associations: Theory and Practice*, Bristol: PARN.

Friedman A.L. and Miles S. (2006). *Stakeholders: Theory and Practice*, Oxford: Oxford University Press.

Friedman A. and Phillips M. (2003). *Governance of Professional Associations: The Players and Processes*, Bristol: PARN.

Friedman A., Phillips M. and Chan M.M. (2002). *Governance of Professional Associations: The Structure and Role of the Governing Body,* Bristol: PARN.

Friedman A., Phillips M. and Cruickshank I. (2002). *The Membership Structures of UK Professional Associations*, Bristol: PARN.

Friedman A. and Williams C. (2006). *Member Relations and Strategy: Supporting Member Involvement and Retention*, Bristol: PARN.

Larson M.S. (1977). *The Rise of Professionalism: A Sociological Analysis*, Berkeley: University of California Press.

Greenwood, R., Suddaby R. and Hinings C.R. (2002). 'Theorizing Change: the role of professional associations in the transformation of institutionalized fields' *Academy of Management Journal*, 45:1, 58-80.

Pugh D.S., Hickson, D.J. and Hinings C.R. (1969). 'An Empirical Taxonomy of Structures of Work Organizations' *Administrative Science Quarterly*, 14:1, 115-126.

Putnam, R. (2000). B*owling Alone: The Collapse and Revival of American Community,* New York: Simon and Schuster.

Macdonald K.M. (1995). *The Sociology of the Professions*, London: SAGE.

PP4SD (Professional Partnerships for Sustainable Development) (2001). A foundation course in sustainable development for professionals, Institution of Environmental Sciences: Bourne, Lincolnshire.

Shoichet, R. (1998). 'An Organization Design Model for Nonprofits', *Nonprofit Management & Leadership*, 9:1, 71-88.

Watkins J., Drury L. and Bray S. (1996). *The Future of the UK Professional Associations*, Cheltenham: Cheltenham Strategic Publications.

Williams C. with Woodhead S. (2007). *The Growing Pains of Smaller Professional Associations: key issues and interesting practice*, Bristol: PARN.

Brundtland G. (ed) (1987). *Our Common Future: The World Commission on Environment and Development*, Oxford: Oxford University Press.

Vetter A. (1998). *The Better Business Pack*, Godalming: WWF-UK.

About PARN Publications

The Professional Associations Research Network (PARN) is a membership organisation dedicated to the support of good practice among professional bodies.

This book is one of many titles available from PARN. A list of titles and the topics covered can be found on our website along with an order form: www.parn.org.uk

RELATED TITLES:

Member Relations and Strategy: Supporting Member Involvement and Retention (2006) By Andy Friedman and Tina Williams
This book offers insights about members, their needs and the requests that they make. It explores the importance of strategy in supporting member relations and considers ways in which professional associations can link member relations to strategy, using feedback cycles which allow both the strategy to inform ways of dealing with members and the experience of interacting with members to influence the strategy. It presents models, tools and processes to strengthen the relationship between strategy and member relations, in order to support member involvement and retention.

2006 – paperback – 136 pages – ISBN 0-9545487-5-2

Analysing Member Services: A Strategic Perspective for Professional Associations (2003) By Andrew Friedman and Jane Mason
This book considers the services provided by professional bodies in a broad context. Based on a comprehensive survey of 340 websites of UK professional associations and membership organisations, it provides a wealth of information on their service offerings. It also provides insights into key issues in developing and marketing services and can be usefully employed by professional associations to facilitate self-reflection, evaluation and benchmarking.

2003 – paperback – 250 pages – ISBN 0-9538347-5-6

Professional Associations in Ireland: A Comparative Study with the UK (2004) By Andrew Friedman and Jane Mason
Second in the series on professionalisation, this book offers a unique comparison of Irish professional associations with UK associations. The subject areas of The Professionalisation of UK Professional Associations are revisited with remarkable findings on topics such as CPD, governance, management, member services, ethical codes, stakeholder relations, public relations and internationalisation of professional associations. PARN's first report focussing on Professional Associations in Ireland provides enlightening information, and a window into the operations of our closest European partners.

2004 – paperback – 104 pages – ISBN 0-9545487-1-X

The Professionalisation of UK Professional Associations: Governance, Management and Member Relations (2004) By Andy Friedman and Jane Mason
This is the first in a series of publications that looks at the professionalisation, or modernisation, of professional associations in the UK and Ireland. We examine the proposition that professional associations are becoming more strategic, more reflective, more structured, in short, more professional. This book concentrates on governance, management and member relations. It incorporates models developed in previous PARN research on governance, membership structures and member services and provides new evidence from a survey amongst 129 professional bodies of the position today. It also includes cases studies of current practice.

2004 – paperback – 147 pages – ISBN 0-9545487-0-1

Other PARN Publications:

In the Governance Series:

Governance of Professional Associations: Theory and Practice (2006)
Governance of Professional Associations: The Players and Processes (2003)
Governance of Professional Associations: The Structure and Role of the Governing Body (2002)

In the Ethics Series:

Analysing Ethical Codes of UK Professional Bodies (2005)
Ethical Codes of UK Professional Associations (2002)
A NEW TITLE ON ETHICAL COMPETENCE WILL BE PUBLISHED IN APRIL 2007

In the CPD Series:

Critical Issues in CPD (2005)
Continuing Professional Development in the UK: Evaluation of Good Practice (2002)
Continuing Professional Development in the UK: Attitudes and Experiences of Practitioners (2001)
Building CPD Networks on the Internet (1999)

Also:
Membership Structures of UK Professional Associations (2002)

To order PARN publications, visit our website: www.parn.org.uk.